Hartstone Inn

Signature Recipes

from an ELEGANT MAINE INN

Janice,

Friends, family and laughter are the best ingredients of all. Happy Cooking!

Michael Salmon

July 2011

CHEF MICHAEL SALMON

Hartstone Inn

Signature Recipes

from an ELEGANT MAINE INN

MICHAEL SALMON

PHOTOGRAPHER: FELICITY COLE ■ CONTRIBUTING WRITER: MICHAELA CAVALLARO

Inquiries should be addressed to:
Michael Salmon
Hartstone Inn
41 Elm Street
Camden, Maine 04843
www.hartstoneinn.com

Author: Michael Salmon
Foreword: Nancy Harmon Jenkins

Library of Congress Control Number: 2003092804

ISBN 0-9729919-0-5

Photographs by Felicity Cole with the following exceptions:
    Alexander Pfotenhauer, pages 4 and 5
    Richard Procopio, pages 3, 12, 20, 33 (photo of Mary Jo), 37, 69, 85,
        135, inside back flap
    Michael Salmon, pages 7, 23, 24, back cover

Designed by: Harrah Lord, Yellow House Studio, Rockport, Maine

Printed by: P. Chan & Edward, Inc.

Printed in China

FIRST EDITION

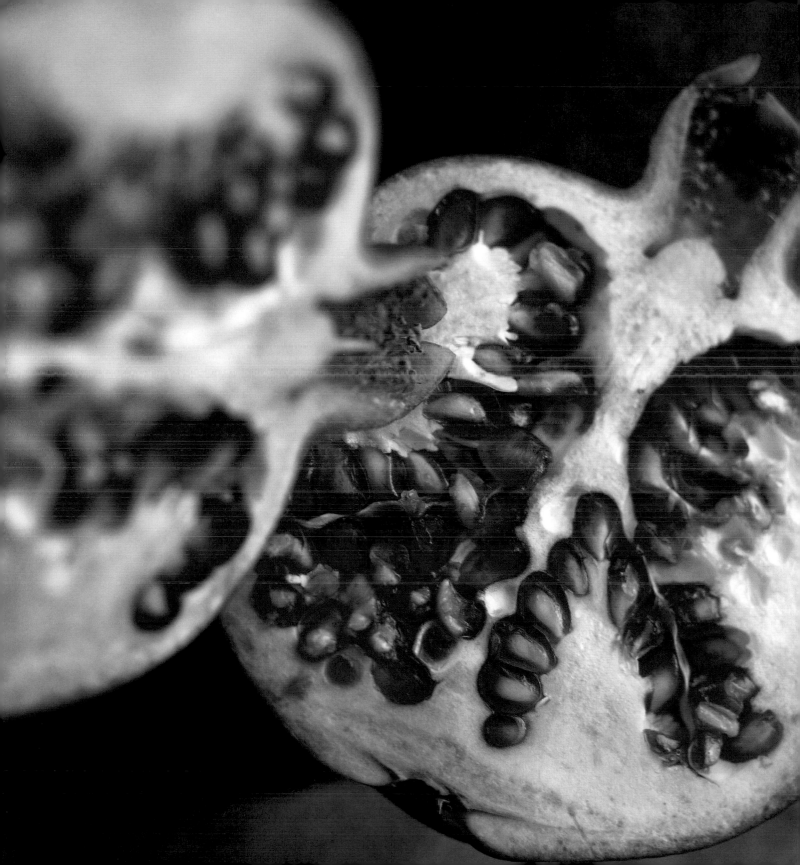

Contents

CONTENTS

$\mathcal{S}$PECIAL ACKNOWLEDGMENT

MY INSPIRATION in life comes from my loving wife Mary Jo. She is my best friend, my business partner, my world. I dedicate this book to her, for without her support and patience, this project would remain a pile on my desk. When we met back in 1987, we knew we had entered into a relationship that was pretty special, a love that would last a lifetime. She knows my thoughts, finishes my sentences and makes me feel complete.

I'D LIKE TO start by thanking the individuals responsible for helping me put this book together. My initial idea for a cookbook was to produce a small 50-page booklet, printed and bound in-house. It would highlight a few of the dishes people have clamored for. My friend Grace Andrews had grander ideas and convinced me to create a book of this caliber. She is always full of good advice.

During one of my cooking classes, the subject of my writing a cookbook came up again. One of the participants, a graphic designer with a good deal of experience in designing books, Harrah Lord, introduced me to a local publisher who liked the idea. That week I also received news that a photographer out of Bermuda, who was planning a trip to Camden, wanted to visit the Inn and take some pictures of the rooms and my food. Felicity Cole has a great eye for food photography, so naturally, I asked her to work on the project. She enthusiastically agreed and returned that fall for two weeks of intense cooking, propping and photography.

Over time, I realized that the publisher and I shared a different vision for the cookbook, so I began to look into self-publishing. I approached Harrah Lord. She not only agreed to produce the book but was also a wealth of information. She walked me through the fascinating process of creating a book, introduced me to an excellent printer and is solely responsible for the layout and design of this book. I am indebted to this versatile and creative woman.

While writing the text for the book, I realized I needed a writer to share another perspective of the Inn. Michaela Cavallaro had written an article on the Hartstone Inn for *Down East* magazine, and I liked her style of writing. So Michaela wrote about the Inn and the local area, and also interviewed and wrote about my purveyors, capturing a bit of their personalities and extracting more than just the usual facts.

By now I had written down and tested all the recipes, had written text for various sections of the book, had gathered all of Michaela's writings and Felicity's photographs. A few key photographs were still missing so a very talented local photographer, Richard Procopio, came to the rescue and produced some amazing shots. Alex Pfotenhauer, another local photographer, shot the exterior of the Inn. The next step—do I or don't I need an editor—was upon me. I'd been encouraged by Harrah to get an editor, but I'd been stalling. I thought it was simply a matter of proofreading, and I had checked the material so many times, I wasn't sure an editor was necessary. Elizabeth IlgenFritz and her husband David Jacobson, frequent guests of ours at the Inn the last year and a half, had recently purchased a home near Camden and were up for a few days when she asked how the book was progressing. I had forgotten that writing, editing and proofreading are her profession. One thing led to another, and after I saw what Elizabeth did to the first page of text, I was sold. The clarity of the writing in this book is due to her talent and hard work.

A book is not complete without a foreword. Nancy Harmon Jenkins is a talented and gifted writer, teacher and cook. She resides in Camden most of the year and freelances for major food magazines and newspapers. Nancy is also the author of several cookbooks on Mediterranean cuisine and recently released her fourth cookbook. In May 2001, Nancy wrote an article for *Food & Wine* magazine on Maine Coast Inns with fine cuisine, and the Hartstone Inn was one of the three inns featured. She has dined with us at the Inn on numerous occasions and even brought Julia Child along one August evening. I am honored that Nancy has written the foreword for this cookbook.

I would also like to thank those people who have assisted us over the years at the Inn. Tim and Sandy La Plante were the first to welcome Mary Jo and me to Camden and to introduce us to the Hartstone Inn. They have provided endless support and inspiration as we learned about innkeeping. Mary Jo's parents Bob and Pat Brink have been involved in many renovations at the Inn, including ripping off and replacing the siding, painting, gardening, basic handyman repairs, and door installation. Pat designed and Bob built the steel chef silhouette that we place in the garden from spring through fall to display our nightly dinner menu. Dennis Hayden and Jody Schmoll, fellow Camden innkeepers, who have become good friends, have assisted and supported us in countless ways. My roommate from culinary school, Scott Prentiss, is a great guy to have around. He has done everything from wallpapering and painting to asphalt cutting and window treatments. His parents Bob and Gail have also been incredibly generous with their time and know-how. Bob claims that anything can be fixed with B-Sealant. When we first took over the Inn, Peter and Donny Smith, former innkeepers in Camden, gave us some climbing roses that brighten the west side of the Inn every summer. Their support and friendship (and the fact that they also gave us two antique crystal chandeliers for the Inn) have meant a lot to us. As an innkeeper, you meet many guests, and through the years some of those guests become close friends. Lisa Haskin is one of these friends. She is also very creative, and a skilled faux painter. She has painted a number of the Inn's rooms, designed and created guest logbooks and menu covers, and has shared with me, and now with you, her recipe for Almond and apricot biscotti. They are to die for. Our friends Peter and Nancy Rice assisted in pouring concrete and setting stones for our front fountain and our local carpenter Armand Lesmerises (Ruthie Perry's father) has been around for every project at the Inn since we began here in 1998. And then there are our wonderful guests at the Inn. Without question, they have supported and inspired every achievement of ours at the Inn. Both Mary Jo and I would like to express our gratitude to you.

I offer a fond thank you to Josh and Ruthie Perry, our assistant innkeepers here at the Inn. They contribute heavily to our success, and their list of responsibilities and accomplishments at the Inn are endless. In addition, Josh assists me in the kitchen on busy evenings during the winter and has become a very good cook. They are truly special people. Lastly, I would like to thank Peter and Elaine (Sunny) Simmons for establishing the Hartstone Inn in 1986. Their hard work and vision turned an old house on Elm Street into the Inn that would fulfill our dreams, and ultimately provide the incentive I needed to create this cookbook. Thank you, one and all.

H

FOREWORD

I GREW UP in Camden at a time when the food was good but plain as all get-out. Garlic was unknown, lemon juice came in a green glass bottle not in a bright yellow fruit and olive oil was something you kept in the medicine closet to rub on babies' scalps. We had the best lobster in the world, of course, and pretty good blueberries, raspberries and apples in season. But we had no adventurous cooks, mostly because we had no adventurous diners.

Times do change, fortunately. And at the Hartstone Inn, Michael and Mary Jo Salmon have been happily in the vanguard of that welcome change, with a cuisine of bold flavors and exciting textures, and a style of presentation that practically defines the understated elegance to which we New Englanders aspire.

The first time I dined at the Hartstone Inn, I was the guest of friends who'd been there many times. A skeptic in the dining room, I was won over immediately by the bright and pretty room, the sparkling table to which we were shown and the elegant place settings, complete with knife rests—knife rests! I hadn't seen them since my grandmother gave up the rigors of Sunday dinner long ago.

There was more to come, however. Because the Hartstone Inn, then and now, was not just a pretty place. As Michael's food began to emerge from the kitchen, plate after plate, course after well-thought-out course, each one was more enticing than the last, each one more pleasing to the eye. We began with a nibble of an amuse-guile, then went on to a seared Chinese five-spice quail with gingered vegetables, proceeded through a cognac-laced lobster bisque and then paused for a peach sorbet, light and refreshing, delicately perfumed with spearmint. Palates cleansed, we continued with a hazelnut-encrusted rack of lamb, and finally, the pièce de résistance, Michael's famous dessert soufflé. If memory serves me, that first one was flavored with mangoes and served with a fragrant vanilla crème anglaise—yes, it makes my mouth water now, in retrospect.

Now, that may sound like a lot of food but there's another aspect to dinner with Michael and Mary Jo—because that's really what dining at the Hartstone Inn is like, dinner with a couple of accomplished and graceful friends—that is just as important and that is the following: It truly is a dining "experience," one to enjoy in the kind of relaxed and leisurely atmosphere that we all long for and find so hard to create in our modern world. Fast food mavens should take note: The Hartstone Inn is not for you! People in a hurry can go up the street to Scott's Place and grab a couple of the finest-kind lobster rolls to eat in their car.

Dining at the Hartstone Inn, on the other hand, is a civilized and civilizing experience. We linger over our meals here, cosseted and comforted, and we are intended to do so, taking the time to savor each dish, to compare flavors and textures and to discuss it with our agreeable hosts. Michael and Mary Jo still serve each dish personally, with a little flourish that indicates they're happy to do so. And we take time between courses as well for the enlightened art of conversation. The evening is spread out before us, an increasingly rare opportunity in our over-pressurized world, to relish in tranquility this unique experience.

And it is indeed unique, not least because Michael is firm in his conviction that the finest local products are the basis of his ingredients. The cuisine is international though rooted in American traditions, ranging from the Caribbean to Thailand and back again. But the ingredients, as much as possible, come from this blessed corner of the coast of Maine.

I hope the readers of this book and the cooks who take it into their own kitchens to use will remember that sense of ease and tranquility that is so much a part of the Hartstone Inn experience. As you read through it and take mental notes of the recipes you want to try—whether it's Michael's homemade granola, the spicy ginger snap cookies or his Thai pork dumplings—keep in mind that dining together is one of the most precious experiences we have as a civilization. At the Hartstone Inn, Michael and Mary Jo Salmon have made that ideal a reality. For that, I thank them and wish them continuing success and good fortune!

Nancy Harmon Jenkins
Camden, March 2003

H

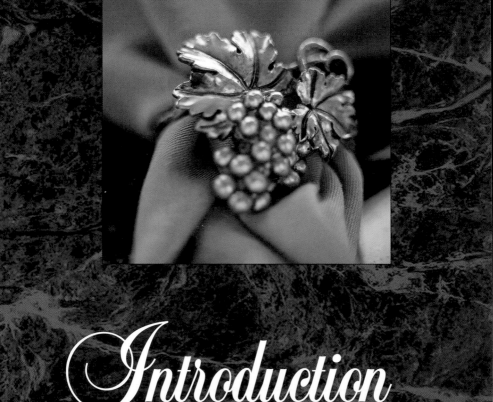

Introduction

Chef Michael Salmon

BOOK CONCEPTION: My culinary experiences over the years have been so diverse that I did not want to limit my cookbook to one specific subject or style of cooking. So, when it came time to develop a concept for my book, I always found myself back at the Hartstone Inn where diversity abounds. I have designed this book around the activities that take place at the Inn, starting with an introduction to my background, the history of the Inn, a tour of the Inn and finally a little about this quaint little village we live in, Camden, Maine.

The recipes gathered in this book range from breakfast and afternoon tea cookies to dinner appetizers, entrées and desserts to highlights from various ethnic cuisines covered in our cooking classes. The cuisine at the Inn touches many cultures and styles of cooking. The breakfast recipes included are some of our favorite morning specialties, ranging from breads and muffins to crepes and frittatas. Afternoon Tea offers cookies, scones and biscotti recipes featured every afternoon at the Inn.

Dinner, of course, presents the greatest opportunity to diversify. With a menu that changes daily, I can utilize the freshest ingredients and combine them with various ethnic techniques to create a five-course menu to be remembered. And so can you. For example, start with a Caribbean appetizer of Annatto grilled shrimp with a pineapple-avocado salsa, follow it with New England corn and lobster chowder, homemade peach sorbet and Olive-encrusted rack of lamb with a rosemary bordelaise. To finish the whole meal off, try one of our famous French-inspired blueberry and hazelnut soufflés with a Frangelico crème anglaise. The cooking classes I offer at the Inn include the five I touch on in this book—Caribbean, Dim Sum, Hors d'Oeuvres, Pasta Pasta Pasta and Thai—and extend beyond into Haute Chinese, Spanish Tapas and Maine seafood. Each year I add a few new courses to the list. All these activities, including the cooking classes, have evolved into written form and become this book.

DEFINING MOMENTS: My first clue that I wanted to be a chef was when I was about 6 years old. I was kneeling in my backyard with my younger brother Tom making mud pies and began envisioning a diner-style cooking line with shiny stainless steel counters and, of all things, a blender. It wasn't until I stopped my paper routes and got a job in a bistro that my desire to become a chef showed itself again.

I was 15 years old working as a dish and pot washer. My sister Colleen who worked as a hostess there had introduced me to Joe, the kitchen manager. Shortly after I began working in the kitchen, the corporate chef for the franchised bistro chain came to my hometown of Rochester, Minnesota, to prepare a small charity dinner at Mayowood, the former estate of William Mayo, co-founder of the Mayo Clinic. My task at this function was to wash pots and dishes and do general cleanup. Joe was there to assist the French chef. I remember the chef opening the trunk of his car and retrieving a tall white chef's toque and a set of kitchen knives. Mayowood was decorated for the Christmas holidays and the grounds were covered with a few feet of freshly fallen snow. As we went to work unpacking the supplies in the rather small kitchen, we quickly ran out of refrigerator space and began sticking things in the snow banks outside the kitchen door for cool storage.

Joe had a great sense of humor, and we kidded around about the chef's thick French accent and his quirks. At one point, the chef sent me outside with a pair of kitchen shears to trim some evergreen boughs, and I wondered why in the world he wanted them. We cut those fragrant evergreens and used them to decorate the passed hors d'oeuvres platters. That really impressed me. Joe and I snickered again from the rear of the kitchen as the chef burned bread in a large sauté pan, at the time not knowing this technique for seasoning a new pan.

My first encounter with a screaming chef happened that evening when he asked for a knife to slice the bread. Here's a chef with a roll of kitchen knives in front of him and he is asking *me* for a bread knife. "Why don't you use one of those?" I asked, pointing to a chef's knife. He screamed, "This is not a bread knife. Where are your knives?" A 15-year-old dish and pot washer and I'm supposed to have knives? When I told him I didn't own any, he asked me which cookbooks I owned and studied. I responded that I was just a dishwasher and wasn't interested in cooking, even though I really was. Somehow he knew this or saw something in me because he said he planned to deduct money from my paycheck and put it toward a set of knives and some cookbooks. I remember being so irate and wondering if he could really garnish my paycheck like that. After all, I had a stereo to buy. By the end of that dinner, I had gained a great deal of respect for the chef and his abilities in the kitchen.

From that moment on, I began spending more time watching and admiring the cooks in the restaurant. In the slow periods, I assisted in peeling onions and washing lettuce. Soon I was promoted to prep cook and learned how to hold and use a chef's knife. I moved to the salad station and slowly worked my way around the kitchen, making soups and quiches, beef bourguignon and chicken coq au vin. Eventually I ran the sauté and grill stations. The summer after I graduated from high school, I went to work in an Italian restaurant down the street, where I learned how to make fresh pasta and many Italian dishes I had never been exposed to. I also took on a part-time position in a local wine shop to learn the basics of wine tasting and appreciation. That fall, I went off to the University of Wisconsin-Stout to study Hotel and Restaurant Management, working part-time in the school's restaurant, and was finally talked into applying to the Culinary Institute of America in New York by a fellow student who had graduated from there himself. During my second year in Wisconsin, I was accepted at the CIA and my parents drove me out to Hyde Park. I was like a sponge at the CIA. Being exposed to so many new techniques and products I had only read about, I found I loved cooking!

I worked weekends at the Hyatt in Greenwich, Connecticut, and when it came time to plan my externship, the chef I worked for arranged a position for me at the Hyatt Regency Grand Cypress near Orlando, Florida. For a young, inspired chef wanna-be, this was the experience of a lifetime. The kitchens were enormous and were filled with talented, driven cooks and chefs who strove for perfection. My time in Florida inspired me as a cook and allowed me to meet the love of my life. Mary Jo had moved to Florida and taken a job at the Hyatt as a restaurant manager just months before I arrived. It was fate.

A year later, back at school in New York, I took a weekend job in Manhattan at the Scandinavian restaurant Aquavit, which is still known as one of the city's premier restaurants. My roommate and I worked about 35 hours each weekend filleting salmon, rolling herring and filling in on various line positions. After graduating from the CIA in October 1988, I moved to Palm Springs, California, to continue my career with Hyatt and to join Mary Jo who had moved there 5 months earlier. I worked in Hyatt kitchens for almost 10 years, including 3 years in Lake Tahoe, where I worked my way up to Executive Sous Chef. While in Tahoe I was also able to go back to college to finish up my bachelor's degree in Hotel, Restaurant and Resort Management, which I had vowed to do. I spent a few years in Atlantic City with Caesar's Hotel and Casino and then 3 years in Aruba with Sonesta Beach Resort Hotel and Casino, where I was Executive Chef of two properties *and* a private island, with a kitchen staff of about 150.

Mary Jo and I had been saving every penny for our dream inn and we decided it was time to move a little closer to that dream. We moved to Windsor, Ontario, to plan the opening of a new casino hotel for the Canadian government, Caesars and Hilton. We spent a little over a year designing restaurant concepts and kitchens, choosing equipment, planning menus, hiring management positions and staff, and organizing seven food and beverage outlets with nearly 1,000 employees. After that huge project, it was finally time to do it for ourselves.

Caribbean Chef of the Year

MARY JO and I spent 3 years on the island of Aruba, working for the Sonesta Beach Resort Hotel and Casino. In 1996, during our time there, the island put together a culinary competition between various hotels and restaurants, and I thought it would be fun to compete. The top five winners (myself included) became the national team for Aruba and went on to compete in a Caribbean-wide competition held in Puerto Rico. There, we competed against 11 other teams—60 chefs in total—from various islands, including Puerto Rico, Jamaica, Cancun, Barbados and Curacao.

The culinary event began with a team competition. Each team went into a kitchen where various food products, including a large pan of tiny fish (a fish not one of my teammates recognized), veal shouders and a bunch of coconuts, were laid out. We had roughly 15 minutes to determine a three-course menu that utilized these ingredients, and about 4 hours to produce the meal for 60 people.

Our menu consisted of a fish appetizer, Aruban style, an island-style veal stew with sweet potatoes served in a plantain basket and a coconut custard dessert. During the first hour, while assisting the pastry chef with dessert, I cut my finger badly while slicing fresh coconut meat on the mandoline. I was able to wrap it and slow the bleeding enough to continue without the judges ever knowing. We went on to win the team competition and were named "Caribbean Team of the Year."

The second part of the event was the individual chef competition, where the five chefs from the top four teams competed against each other. In the middle of a large ballroom, these 20 chefs had one hour to prepare a single dish for four people. There were two tasting judges, a performance judge and a photographer who photographed the plate presentation. During the entire hour, each chef was judged on every detail, from knife skills to cooking techniques to cleanliness to the actual timing of the final dish. My dish (the recipe can be found on page 100) was Plantain shrimp with a passion fruit-annatto sauce and mango salsa. I felt good about my performance, but with such talented competitors, I had not expected to win the two gold medals at the closing ceremony that evening.

Food & Wine magazine and American Express sponsored the competition, and awarded me with the two medals and two colorful plates naming me both a member of the "Caribbean Team of the Year" and "Caribbean Chef of the Year" for 1996–1997. It was quite an honor, and was topped off with a nice article in a special section of *USA Today* on November 8, 1996.

The Historical Hartstone Inn

THE GRACIOUS HOME that eventually became the Hartstone Inn was built in 1835 for Joseph C. Stetson, a Camden, Maine, merchant. The widow Rosy Stone, whose husband had also been a doctor, bought the two-story, Federal-style house in 1882, and owned it until the early 1890s. Mrs. Stone sold the home to Dr. Willis F. Hart and his wife Mary Adelaide Gilmore Hart. Soon after, the Harts added a mansard roof, popular during the period for converting an attic into usable living quarters. This renovation was completed just before the great fire that decimated much of Camden's downtown.

In the middle of the night on November 10, 1892, the fire started in the basement of a building on North Elm Street. By the time it burned out, 60 businesses and 18 homes had been destroyed. Within the next year, downtown Camden was entirely rebuilt—this time primarily out of brick. According to local lore, as the fire worked its way toward their house on South Elm Street, Mrs. Hart had all her valuable furniture carried out to the yard to save it from the approaching fire. Ironically, the house was saved, but much of the furniture had been ruined, scorched by glowing embers.

Their home, located on what became known as "Doctors' Row," was also Dr. Hart's office. The doctor continued to renovate the house, adding Victorian touches like the vestibule and bay windows. Perhaps his most unusual and creative renovation was the turnstile he had installed in the barn. When he came home from a house call, he unhitched the horse and, using the turnstile, turned the carriage around so it faced the street, ready for his next call.

To this day, Dr. Hart's descendants, including his grandson John Hart, still live in the Camden area. In fact, John and Nellie Hart recently celebrated their 50th wedding anniversary at the Inn, where their wedding ceremony had also taken place.

In 1986, Peter and Sunny Simmons, a former official with the New York State Lottery and the proprietor of a retail business in the Caribbean, respectively, turned the house into an inn, naming it after its former owners. Over much of the next 12 years, they converted the house from home to inn. And in 1998, the Simmons turned the Hartstone Inn over to its current proprietors, Michael and Mary Jo Salmon.

Our History at the Inn

FROM THE BEGINNING, Michael and Mary Jo knew they wanted to have an inn of their own. So even as they advanced up the corporate ladder, they spent their vacations investigating potential locations for a cozy inn. The former Midwesterners—Michael is from Minnesota and Mary Jo is from central Michigan—found that they were enthralled with New England. In 1993, they began scheduling their vacations around the Fourth of July—not a bad time of year to escape Aruba, after all—and explored Cape Cod, Newburyport, Exeter and Portsmouth, among other towns and cities along the Atlantic coast. Somewhat to their surprise, the further north they went, the happier they became.

And then they experienced Camden, Maine. Despite their arrival on a night so foggy they didn't even know Mt. Battie existed, Michael and Mary Jo fell in love with the sophisticated little town on Penobscot Bay. After another two years, and a move from Aruba to Windsor, Ontario, the Salmons were ready to take the plunge.

In the summer of 1997, they called innkeepers they knew in Camden, who mentioned that a wonderful property was on the market, one the innkeepers would have bought if they'd been looking. From there, events kicked into high gear. A week later, Michael and Mary Jo made the 14-hour drive from Windsor to Camden. They spent the weekend looking at properties including the Hartstone Inn, where they spent one night. Everything about the inn appealed to them—its location, the size, the style and the potential. Before the weekend had ended, they'd signed an agreement to buy the Hartstone Inn.

The drive back to Ontario flew by. Michael and Mary Jo planned the name and theme of every guest room in the Inn. They made a list of what they would use to decorate each room. They discussed Mary Jo's concept to turn the Inn's country-style décor into a model of Victorian elegance that would take advantage of the many antiques and collectibles she and Michael had gathered over the years in anticipation of this event.

The following May, Michael and Mary Jo took over the Inn's operations and began renovating in earnest. The first big project was the addition of the dining porch—to add more tables for Michael's long-awaited dinner service. When finished, the dining porch seamlessly matched the building's original style. The next year, Michael undertook another pleasing project—the expansion and complete remodeling of his kitchen. He had been working in a kitchen so small that the dirty dishes from one course had to be stacked on the counter in order to make room to plate the next. The new kitchen is double the size and is dominated by a vast center island that not only provides ample room for plating between courses but also comfortably hosts Michael's cooking classes.

After Michael and Mary Jo's second season, with the addition of the dining porch and the expansion of the kitchen, the Hartstone Inn began to welcome the public to the gourmet five-course dinner, which previously had been available only to registered guests.

Michael and Mary Jo renovated every room in the Inn, adding stylish wallpaper and new walls to gas fireplaces and luxurious bathrooms. Recently, they redecorated two suites in the rear of the building with marble bathrooms, head board wainscoting and airy skylights, and created a third suite from the former owners' quarters. Michael and Mary Jo undertake these renovations with sophistication, relaxation and comfort in mind. An upcoming project involves moving the bathroom of the cozy Tally-Ho room so guests no longer need to dash across the hall in their bathrobes to use the facilities. With the completion of that project, each of the guest rooms will include its own private bathroom, entered from the privacy of one's room.

A Tour of the Inn

MARY JO AND MICHAEL have decorated each guest room at the Hartstone Inn in keeping with the room's theme—and the guests' comfort. The beds, many of them four-poster, are piled with big down pillows and dressed with stylish coordinating

linens. White noise machines and wooden massagers can be found on every dresser, and a small pair of scissors hangs on the wall from tassels Mary Jo bought in Italy. Inspiration for a pair of scissors in every guest room came after guests with price tags on items purchased at L.L. Bean needed to borrow the Inn's scissors again and again. (L.L. Bean is in Freeport, west on Route 1, about an hour from the Inn.)

The Mansard Suite celebrates 17th-century French architect Francois Mansart, for whom the high-pitched, two-sloped roof of the Inn is named. To be faithful to Mansart's heritage, the windows are dressed with hand-tied French lace curtains and the room itself is accented by Michael and Mary Jo's collection of Quimper china.

British details accentuate cozy **Tally Ho,** where a red brick fireplace and equestrian prints create a clubby atmosphere. The queen-sized, four-poster cherry bed is dressed with a Ralph Lauren duvet, and the wallpaper, an intense paisley of deep brown, navy, dark green and burgundy is the perfect complement to this charming room.

Wedgwood is decorated with blue Jasperware Wedgwood and prints collected by Michael and Mary Jo in England and Ireland. Under the ornate high ceiling, the queen-sized canopy bed is dressed in beautiful linens of ivory and Wedgwood blue.

Magnolia, one of the first rooms reinvigorated when Michael and Mary Jo took over the Hartstone Inn, features a soothing array of soft colors, with a four-poster,

queen-sized bed and a handmade Amish lace canopy. The original marble sink stands in the bathroom and a fireplace warms the inviting sitting area.

The theme of **Victorian Charm,** a spacious front corner room with two comfortable chairs lit by a Tiffany-style lamp in the reading area, was inspired by the elegant bay window that overlooks Elm Street. Roses dominate the room, which is home to a queen-sized iron bed with brass accents and romantic Laura Ashley bedding.

One of the most inviting aspects of cozy **Lark's Nest** is its Victorian claw-foot tub. In addition, the fireplace, hardwood floors and comfortable Victorian décor make this room a hard one to leave.

The Teacup Suite is home to one of Mary Jo's most personal collections—antique teacups her grandmother began collecting for her when Mary Jo was a toddler. Displayed on shelves built by Mary Jo's grandfather, they provide a quiet elegance to this corner suite. The skylight above the queen-sized bed encourages stargazing while its warm fireplace inspires romance.

Mary Jo's remarkable orchids inspired the décor of the aptly named **Orchid Room,** which Dr. Hart, who owned the home in the early 20th century, used as his office. Today, the room's subtle paisley-patterned walls display artful orchid prints that complement its crisp blue-and-white color scheme.

The Cottage Suite, once the owners' quarters, is a lovely retreat. The Brazilian hardwood floors, warmly painted walls, exposed beams and hand-painted Quimper china create a sophisticated French-cottage feel in the living room that offers a lovely sitting area with fireplace. Luxuriate in the jacuzzi tub in the step-down bathroom or listen to the tranquil fountain in your private garden of wildflowers outside the windows of the richly appointed bedroom.

The Garden Suite couldn't be more comfortable. It overlooks scenic Mt. Battie, and is decorated in keeping with its natural theme. Located in what was once the carriage house, the suite's entrance is private, and its bi-level design provides a spacious bedroom and bath upstairs and a delightful sitting area with tiled entry downstairs.

Guests who stay in the **Mt. Battie Suite** will enjoy the Inn's most recent renovation. A tiled entry, bead board wainscoting, exposed beams and a skylight add to the cottage feel of this charming suite. Soothing green and white toile walls, plush Berber carpet and a luxurious king-sized bed dressed with beautiful muted browns and white designer linens provide a quietly elegant air to this bi-level suite with private entrance.

Michael and Mary Jo approach the Hartstone Inn's common areas with the same attention to detail and comfort. In the parlor, the original marble fireplace and bay window are accented by rich burgundy walls, a color chosen by Mary Jo to create a Victorian-influenced and luxurious atmosphere. Clearly, her concept works. Peek in the door of the bright, cheerful room during the morning and you're likely to see a guest curled on a sofa gazing at several varieties of orchids or admiring the portraits of Dr. and Mrs. Willis Hart, who owned the home at the turn of the century. In the early evening, diners gather in the parlor for a convivial glass of wine before being escorted to the dining room for an extraordinary dinner.

Across the hall, the library, with its dark cherry wood cabinets, hunter-green wallpaper and Queen Anne leather club chairs with dark cherry legs, is a cozy spot for afternoon tea and cookies or a friendly game of chess. Michael and Mary Jo have stocked the bookshelves with local histories, travel guides, poetry collections, novels and movies for guest room VCRs. The library is also home to part of Michael and Mary Jo's extensive collection of current magazines that reflects their interest in cooking, sailing, gardening and decorating.

Beyond the library's French doors is the original dining room, complete with a working fireplace and a crystal chandelier hung by Michael just days before the Inn opened. It connects to the dining porch via a pocket door where a window once existed—and where the window's original molding stands to this day. The dining porch itself looks as though it were original to the building, which was Michael's goal when he designed it. Michael and Mary Jo's personal china collection is arranged in the china cabinet, and the English Portmeirion china they discovered in England is displayed on a plate rail above the entrance. Dinner tables are set with elegant, white Schonwald china from Germany that displays Michael's culinary creations to perfection, as well as cut crystal knife rests from Hungary, crystal candlesticks, fine silver, fresh flowers and napkin rings from Mary Jo's collection, some of which are gifts from long-time guests.

The kitchen is home to another personal collection, Michael's antique chocolate molds, which is displayed on a rail around the room. The room is a chef's delight, complete with a hanging pot rack for the copper pans Michael and Mary Jo carried by hand from Paris, basket drawers for onions and potatoes and a baking station with pullout drawers for flour, sugar and other necessities.

The Inn's Gardens

EARLY ON, Michael and Mary Jo decided to make gardens a prominent part of the Hartstone Inn experience. Michael convinced an old friend from culinary school to help him tear out the front driveway and in its place create the lovely garden guests see from the dining porch. In the garden's design, Michael and Mary Jo were inspired by their visits to the Cotswold region of England, known for its wild gardens.

From the beginning, the couple has taken a trial-and-error approach to creating the garden's blooms. The first year, Mary Jo remembers with a laugh, they got the colors right, but the layout and design needed some fine-tuning. Today, the garden is tiered, with an ever-changing array of seasonal blooms that keep it attractive from the late Maine spring through the gorgeous New England autumn. Michael and Mary Jo commit a few long days in the fall to planting nearly 500 bulbs for the following spring, and Mary Jo spends some of her winter downtime perusing catalogs to find the long-blooming varieties that keep the gardens bright.

In the back of the Inn, Michael tends an herb garden he inherited from Sunny Simmons, the Inn's previous owner. The sage, tarragon, oregano and mint have been growing there for years. Each spring, Michael supplements them with annual herbs like basil, cilantro and dill and continues to expand his perennial herb garden. The herbs make their way to diners' plates over the summer and sometimes into early winter, when fresh-picked sage enlivens the Thanksgiving turkey.

Many plants in the Inn's gardens are reminders to Michael and Mary Jo of special people in their lives. The climbing rose bushes on the west side of the Inn were a gift from fellow Camden innkeepers to commemorate their purchase of the Hartstone Inn. Members of the couple's families have begun giving them gifts of plants and bulbs, and a few returning guests have made their own contributions—cuttings from their home gardens for a permanent spot at the Inn.

Mary Jo's Passion for Orchids

MARY JO'S fascination with orchids evolved during the years she and Michael spent in Aruba, where she developed a collection of the exotic, captivating plants that grow so well in the tropics. When it came time to leave Aruba, Mary Jo reluctantly left the orchids behind, giving them back to the local woman who had introduced her to them.

But her interest in the plants continued to expand. In the year Michael and Mary Jo spent in Canada before buying the Hartstone Inn, Mary Jo amassed 50 new orchids—plants the couple moved from Ontario to Camden in the back of their Jeep Cherokee, along with their two cats. The more Mary Jo read about orchids, the more orchids she acquired. As her collection neared 100, the Inn began to resemble a jungle. However, the large number meant Mary Jo could rotate the plants in order to have blooming orchids in the Inn's common areas year-round.

Today, Mary Jo has about 400 orchids. When they're not at the Inn, the orchids reside in a custom greenhouse, complete with humidity system, water storage tanks and an automatic heat and ventilation system, that Michael built for his wife. Mary Jo's orchid expertise has led to the Inn's newest creation—Orchid Lovers' weekends, which include a tour of the greenhouse, instruction on the care and feeding of orchids and an orchid plant to take home.

Welcome to Camden, Maine

THE CAMDEN HOME of the Hartstone Inn is beloved for its local artists and craftspeople, eclectic shops, diverse restaurants and a compact downtown that's easy to get around on foot. But the jewel of Camden's historic downtown, much of which was built in the renewal following the fire of 1892, is the harbor—one of the prettiest in all of Maine. The Public Landing is a short walk from the Hartstone Inn's front steps. There, on the docks of Camden Harbor, you can watch tall-masted schooners tie up between excursions in the Gulf of Maine. A two-hour tour on the schooner *Surprise* is a delightful way to spend a morning, learning natural history and local lore from Captain Jack and his wife Barbara, and perhaps helping to hoist a sail yourself. Sea kayaking in Camden harbor and on various area lakes is a wonderful way to spend a morning or afternoon. Several local companies lead kayak tours and provide all of the necessary equipment, including Riverdance Outfitters, owned and operated by our assistants Josh and Ruthie Perry.

North of Camden proper is the lovely and scenic Camden Hills State Park, home to Mt. Battie. There are hiking trails for all abilities as well as the Mt. Battie Auto Road for those who prefer to reach the top by car. The view from the summit is spectacular, and well worth the small admission charge. Winter visitors will find the cross-country skiing breathtaking. In the summer, nearby Lake Megunticook is a perfect spot for bass fishing or lounging on the grass to watch the local rock climbers on Maiden Cliff.

It's an easy drive 25 miles north to Searsport, where the Penobscot Marine Museum displays marine paintings, artifacts and ship models from a 19th-century fishing village. Along the way, stop in downtown Belfast, once home to chicken processing plants and shoe factories, and now a charming, revitalized community with interesting architecture, shopping and beautiful old homes.

To the south of Camden you'll find even more to do. The Camden Snow Bowl has hosted winter recreation for residents since 1936; today it's a premier location for world-class tobogganing and the only spot in the East where you can ski the slopes while enjoying amazing ocean vistas. Rockland's Farnsworth Museum displays American art from all eras, specializing in the works of N.C., Andrew and James Wyeth. A bit further south, the Owl's Head Transportation Museum is filled with a fascinating collection of antique automobiles, airplanes, engines, bicycles and carriages.

Breakfast at the Inn

GUESTS HAVE written again and again in the journals provided in each room at the Hartstone Inn that waking up at the Inn is like returning to childhood and a treasured grandmother's home. Guests may rise to the irresistible smells of bacon, Green Mountain coffee and bread in the oven. But unless you happened to have a grandmother who treated you to multiple-course breakfasts and fresh-blended juices, that's where the similarity ends. Guests wander into the dining room from 8:30 to 9:15. The long seating means diners can wait for a private table if they prefer, rather than sit with other guests. The atmosphere is casual and friendly. The dining porch and dining room are sunny and bright, and the table settings are whimsical, with each guest's breakfast served on a different design from Mary Jo's collection of Portmeirion botanicals.

Michael's goal is to create dishes the average person doesn't usually enjoy for breakfast. Mary Jo greets morning diners with glasses of freshly blended juices, such as banana-strawberry or pineapple-passion fruit, and cups of steaming coffee, complete with individual pitchers of cream and lump sugar imported from France. The starter course often involves fruit—a Poached pear with a raspberry-star anise sauce, Berry crepes or homemade cranberry granola. And as a starter should, it whets the appetite for what's to follow. For the benefit of those staying more than one night, Michael alternates the breakfast entrée between savory and sweet. Guests might enjoy Prosciutto baked eggs, smoked salmon benedict or a Lobster and asparagus quiche while the sweet entrées might be Maine blueberry and almond pancakes or Belgian waffles with fresh fruit. The seasons influence Michael's plans for breakfast as much as they do dinner. Summer guests are apt to experience Maine's abundant berry crop and those who arrive in autumn may find local apples on their plates.

As guests discuss what to do, Mary Jo offers assistance, from giving detailed directions to helping plan excursions. Often one table of guests wonders out loud if they should take a schooner ride and visitors who already did so will offer firsthand details. Between Mary Jo's recommendations and Michael's wonderful meal, guests set off fully prepared.

Once guests have gotten a taste of Michael's cooking, and a glimpse of his approach to dining, breakfast is also the time when those who haven't already made reservations for a gourmet dinner at the Hartstone Inn tend to do so.

BREAKFAST AT THE INN

ucchini Bread

MAKES 4 SMALL LOAVES

3 LARGE EGGS
3/4 CUP CANOLA OIL
2 CUPS GRANULATED SUGAR
2 TEASPOONS VANILLA EXTRACT
2 3/4 CUPS ALL-PURPOSE FLOUR
1 TEASPOON SALT
1 1/2 TEASPOONS BAKING SODA
1 TEASPOON CINNAMON
1/2 CUP WHOLE MILK
2 CUPS GRATED ZUCCHINI (1 LARGE ZUCCHINI)
1 CUP WALNUT PIECES

Zucchini bread has always been one of my favorites. This recipe produces a moist cake, and the walnuts give it a great crisp texture. Thick slices of the zucchini bread can be dipped into beaten eggs and fried in butter creating a unique twist to French toast. Serve with pure maple syrup and freshly whipped cream. The zucchini bread batter can also be used to make muffins. ■

1. Preheat the oven to 350 degrees.

2. Beat together the eggs, oil, sugar and vanilla in a mixer.

3. Combine the flour, salt, baking soda and cinnamon together in a separate bowl and mix. Add into mixer and combine with the egg mixture. Add milk, zucchini and nuts and fold in by hand.

4. Brush four small loaf pans (2 1/2 cup size) with butter and lightly coat with flour, tapping out excess flour.

5. Pour batter into loaf pans (fill 3/4 full) and bake until a toothpick comes out clean, about 1 hour.

6. Remove from the oven and let cool 5 minutes. Transfer the loaves to cooling racks to cool.

LEMON-POPPY SEED MUFFINS

MAKES 20 MUFFINS

3 CUPS ALL-PURPOSE FLOUR
1 1/2 TEASPOONS SALT
1 1/2 TEASPOONS BAKING POWDER
1 1/2 CUPS GRANULATED SUGAR
2 TABLESPOONS POPPY SEEDS
3 LARGE EGGS
1 1/2 CUPS WHOLE MILK
1 CUP CANOLA OIL
1 1/2 TEASPOONS LEMON EXTRACT
1/2 LEMON (GRATED ZEST AND JUICE)

1. Preheat the oven to 350 degrees.

2. Mix together the flour, salt, baking powder, sugar and poppy seeds. Add the remaining ingredients and mix well.

3. Brush muffin tins with butter and lightly coat with flour, tapping out excess flour.

4. Pour the batter into the muffin tins, filling about 3/4 full, and bake until a toothpick comes out clean, about 25 minutes.

5. Remove from the oven and let cool 3 minutes. Transfer the muffins to racks to cool.

I make these muffins a lot at the Inn. The batter can also be used in small loaf pans to create small loaves of bread. The moist citrus cake is a perfect accompaniment for breakfast and is also great in the afternoon with tea. I often substitute other citrus flavors like mandarins or tangerines for the lemons. A splash of Grand Marnier or Cointreau will add another taste dimension to this recipe. ■

PISTACHIO POUND CAKE

MAKES 2 SMALL LOAVES

1 CUP, PLUS 1 TABLESPOON GRANULATED SUGAR

1 CUP UNSALTED BUTTER, SOFT

4 LARGE EGGS

1 TEASPOON VANILLA EXTRACT

1³/4 CUPS ALL-PURPOSE FLOUR

1/2 CUP CRACKED PISTACHIOS (PLUS 1 TABLESPOON FOR
    THE TOP)

1. Preheat the oven to 350 degrees.

2. Cream the sugar and butter together in a mixer until smooth.

3. Add the eggs and vanilla and mix in. Add the flour and ¹/2 cup of pistachios and mix until incorporated.

4. Butter two small loaf pans (2¹/2 cup size) and lightly coat with flour, tapping out the excess flour. Divide the batter between the two pans and sprinkle the tops with the remaining pistachios. Bake until a toothpick comes out clean, about 1 hour.

5. Remove from the oven and let cool 5 minutes. Transfer the loaves to cooling racks to cool.

I have made many different pound cakes over the years, but the flavor, color and texture that the pistachios lend to this cake are incredible. Pound cake is terrific served with afternoon tea also. If you don't eat nuts, the pistachios may be omitted from the recipe. Experiment with other nuts or other flavors like citrus, blueberries or chopped dried fruits. ∎

Fresh Berry Crepes

SERVES 8

CREPE BATTER

2 LARGE EGGS
1/2 CUP COLD WATER
1/2 CUP WHOLE MILK
1/4 TEASPOON SALT
3/4 CUP ALL-PURPOSE FLOUR
2 TABLESPOONS UNSALTED BUTTER, MELTED
CANOLA OIL FOR FRYING PAN

This recipe serves 8 as a first course with one crepe per person. If you want to serve these as the main dish in the morning or as a dessert at night, 2 crepes per person may be more appropriate. Stir things up a little by substituting other fruits for the berries. Try chopped fresh nectarines, mangoes or cherries—almost any fruit will do—and match it with a coordinating crème anglaise. ■

1. In a blender, combine the eggs, water, milk and salt. Blend briefly at medium speed to combine. Add the flour and blend. After the flour has been thoroughly incorporated, with the blender still going at medium speed, add the melted butter in a slow stream, and blend until combined. Refrigerate for 1 hour.

2. To make the crepes, you can either use a crepe pan (follow the instructions that came with the pan) or a plain 10-inch nonstick skillet. Heat the pan on medium heat and add a small splash of oil. Ladle 2 ounces (1/4 cup) of batter into the pan and tip the pan to spread the batter evenly across the bottom of the pan in a thin layer. Cook briefly on this side until it lightly browns and then flip it over (you can use a rubber spatula to assist with this) to cook the other side for 30 seconds.

3. Remove from pan and layer on a plate, repeating with the remaining batter and a little oil in the pan. Recipe makes about ten 8-inch crepes. Keep covered with plastic until needed.

BERRY PASTRY CREAM

    2 CUPS WHOLE MILK
    ¼ CUP CORNSTARCH
    ¼ CUP GRANULATED SUGAR
    ¼ TEASPOON SALT
    2 LARGE EGGS
    ½ TEASPOON VANILLA EXTRACT
    2 CUPS FRESH BERRIES, SLICE STRAWBERRIES
       IF USING THEM (RESERVE HALF FOR GARNISH)
    2 TABLESPOONS UNSALTED BUTTER, SOFT
    RASPBERRY CRÈME ANGLAISE (RECIPE, PAGE 55)

1. Heat the milk to a simmer in a medium-sized saucepan, set over medium heat.

2. In a bowl, whisk together the cornstarch, sugar and salt. Whisk in the eggs.

3. When the milk reaches the simmer, slowly temper the egg mixture by whisking some of the hot milk into the egg mixture. After half of the milk has been added to the egg mixture, whisk the egg mixture back into the remaining milk in the saucepan over medium heat. Whisk constantly until the pastry cream becomes really thick. Cook for 2 minutes after the mixture starts to bubble, stirring constantly. Transfer mixture to a bowl and let cool. Mix in the vanilla and berries. *Pastry cream will keep for one week in the refrigerator.*

TO CONSTRUCT: Lay the crepes out on the counter good side down. Divide the pastry cream equally among the crepes and spread it around evenly with a thin spatula or table knife. Fold the crepes in quarters and place on a lightly buttered baking sheet. Brush the top of each crepe with a little soft butter. Bake the crepes in a 350-degree oven for about 10 minutes (to heat through). Serve one crepe in the middle of a plate drizzled with Raspberry crème anglaise and dusted with powdered sugar. Sprinkle with the remaining fresh berries and finish with a sprig of fresh spearmint.

POACHED PEARS WITH A RASPBERRY-STAR ANISE SAUCE

SERVES 4

1 LEMON
1 CUP LIGHT CORN SYRUP
1 CUP GRANULATED SUGAR
1 STICK CINNAMON BARK
2 WHOLE STAR ANISE
¼ CUP RED WINE
¼ CUP RASPBERRIES, FRESH OR FROZEN
1 CUP ORANGE JUICE
2 FIRM/RIPE BOSC PEARS
4 SLICES OF PISTACHIO POUND CAKE (RECIPE, PAGE 43)
RASPBERRY-STAR ANISE SAUCE (RECIPE, PAGE 48)
CRÈME ANGLAISE (RECIPE, PAGE 55)

1. With a vegetable peeler, remove strips of the yellow outer zest from the lemon. Juice the lemon. Place the lemon juice and zest in a small saucepan with the corn syrup, sugar, cinnamon stick, star anise, red wine, raspberries and orange juice. Bring the poaching liquid to a boil, and reduce the heat to a simmer.

2. Peel the pears, cut in half and core with a melon baller. Poach the pears for 15 minutes or until tender. Remove and let cool slightly.

3. Slice pears on the diagonal and fan out over a slice of the Pistachio pound cake. Top with a few Tablespoons of Raspberry-star anise sauce, dust with powdered sugar, and ladle a little Crème anglaise around the perimeter of the plate.

Poached pears are a nice light breakfast starter. When you are finished poaching the pears, strain and cool the poaching liquid and store in a covered container in the refrigerator. This liquid can be kept for 2 weeks, and used as many times as you would like. The more fruit you poach in the liquid, the more flavorful it becomes. I also serve the poached pears over the Lemon-poppy seed bread (recipe, page 41).

RASPBERRY-STAR ANISE SAUCE

Fresh summer berries can be used in this recipe, but frozen ones work just as well. If you use frozen berries, get the IQF (Individually Quick Frozen) berries. Other varieties of berries work equally as well in this sauce. Blueberries and boysenberries can be directly substituted for the raspberries, while strawberries should be finely chopped before being added. If you don't care for the anise flavor, substitute a few cinnamon sticks. ■

1 CUP GRANULATED SUGAR

3 WHOLE STAR ANISE

1 TABLESPOON, PLUS 1 TEASPOON CORNSTARCH

1/2 VANILLA BEAN, CUT IN HALF LENGTHWISE (OR 1/4 TEASPOON VANILLA EXTRACT)

1 CUP WATER

1 LEMON, JUICE AND ZEST

2 CUPS RASPBERRIES, FRESH OR FROZEN

1. In a small saucepan, combine the sugar, star anise and cornstarch. Mix well. Finely mince the lemon zest. Scrape the vanilla beans from the pod and add both to the pan with the water, lemon juice and lemon zest. Mix well.

2. Bring to a boil over medium heat, reduce the heat and simmer for 5 minutes. Fish out the star anise and vanilla pod and discard. Stir in the raspberries. Return to a boil and cool.

Stone-Ground Grains
from Morgan's Mills

IN A WATER-POWERED mill celebrating its 200th birthday in 2003, Richard Morgan carefully grinds whole grain flour with a combination of modern technology and ancient techniques. He bought the then-abandoned mill in Union, Maine, in 1978. Using the skills he honed as a machinist, he upgraded the equipment and transformed the belts-and-pulleys system into a modern hydroelectric facility. Now, water from Morgan's 700-acre reservoir creates electricity to power the mill; what's left over gets sold into Maine's electrical grid.

The renewable energy is a terrific side benefit of Morgan's main enterprise—grinding whole grains into flavorful, nutritious flour that's distributed throughout New England, and around the world. The grinding method he uses is a process he learned while working as a farmhand on ranches that grew organic wheat and barley in the upland valleys of Colorado, where he was raised. Unlike the extended shelf life of bleached and enriched flour you find in every supermarket in the country, Morgan's Mills flour has a 6-month shelf life. His three-person staff keeps "every kind of grain you could imagine" on hand and grinds it to order between sharp granite stones. At the Hartstone Inn, Michael uses only Morgan's Mills whole grains for the delicious granola he created for the Inn's guests.

Hartstone Granola

Our granola has become one of our signature breakfast starters. Many people ask to buy bags of it to take home with them. I have done that on occasion after a fresh batch comes out of the oven, but by sharing this recipe with you here, you won't have to wait until your next trip to the Inn to have a bowl.

6 CUPS OLD-FASHIONED OATS
1 1/2 CUPS WHEAT GERM
1 CUP WHEAT BRAN
1 CUP OAT BRAN
1 CUP SLICED ALMONDS
1 CUP WALNUT PIECES
2 CUPS BROWN SUGAR, FIRMLY PACKED
2 CUPS SHREDDED COCONUT
3/4 CUP SESAME SEEDS
1/2 CUP SUNFLOWER SEEDS
1 CUP DRIED POWDERED MILK
1/2 CUP HONEY
1/2 CUP MAPLE SYRUP
1/2 CUP CANOLA OIL
2 TEASPOONS VANILLA EXTRACT
1 CUP RAISINS
1 CUP DRIED CRANBERRIES

1. Preheat the oven to 350 degrees.

2. Spread the oats out on two baking sheets with sides and toast for 15 minutes.

3. Mix together the remaining grains, nuts, brown sugar, coconut, sesame seeds, sunflower seeds and dry milk in a large bowl.

4. In a small bowl, mix together the honey, maple syrup, oil and vanilla extract.

5. When the oats are toasted, add them to the large bowl with the grains along with the honey mixture and mix well. Spread the mixture out on the two baking sheets and bake for 15 minutes, stirring occasionally.

6. Remove from the oven and mix in the cranberries and raisins. *Cool and store in an airtight container, for up to 1 month.*

MAINE BLUEBERRY AND ALMOND PANCAKES

Mary Jo says that my pancakes are almost as good as her Grandma Dorothy's, which is quite a compliment having tasted a few of her creations myself. My pancakes get really crisp around the edges and are rather dense, just the way I like them. The blueberries can be easily omitted and replaced with sliced bananas and walnuts or homemade granola or just served plain. However you prepare them, always serve them with pure maple syrup. ■

SERVES 4

1 3/4 CUPS ALL-PURPOSE FLOUR
2 TEASPOONS BAKING POWDER
3/4 TEASPOON SALT
1/4 CUP ALMOND PASTE
2 LARGE EGGS, SEPARATED
2 CUPS WHOLE MILK
1/4 CUP UNSALTED BUTTER, MELTED
1/2 TEASPOON ALMOND EXTRACT
1/2 TEASPOON VANILLA EXTRACT
1 CUP BLUEBERRIES (PREFERABLY WILD MAINE BLUEBERRIES)
POWDERED SUGAR
SLICED ALMONDS, TOASTED

1. Mix dry ingredients (flour, baking powder and salt) in a bowl. In a mixer, beat together the almond paste and egg yolks. Add milk and mix. Stir in the dry ingredients. Add melted butter and extracts and mix. Fold in the blueberries.

2. Beat egg whites until stiff. Fold egg whites into the batter gently, just until combined.

3. Pour batter, 1/4 cup per pancake, onto a hot griddle. Cook until browned on the first side, flip and continue to cook the other side.

4. Place the pancakes on a serving plate and garnish by sprinkling with powdered sugar and toasted almonds. Serve with Chicken sausage patties (recipe follows) and pure Maine maple syrup.

CHICKEN SAUSAGE PATTIES

SERVES 8 (TWO PATTIES EACH)

1 POUND CHICKEN BREAST, BONELESS AND SKINLESS
2 TABLESPOONS OLIVE OIL
1/4 CUP FINELY CHOPPED YELLOW ONION
1/4 CUP FINELY CHOPPED RED BELL PEPPER
1/2 TEASPOON FRESHLY GROUND BLACK PEPPER
1/2 TEASPOON FENNEL SEEDS, GROUND
1 TEASPOON KOSHER SALT
2 TEASPOONS FRESHLY CHOPPED PARSLEY
1 LARGE EGG
2 TABLESPOONS HEAVY CREAM
2 TABLESPOONS OLIVE OIL

1. Remove any tendons and cartilage from the chicken breast, and cut into 1/4 inch cubes.

2. Heat 2 Tablespoons olive oil in a small sauté pan set over medium-high heat, and add the onions. Cook for 1 minute, stirring, and add the chopped red bell pepper. Cook for 30 seconds, stirring, and remove from heat. Cool.

3. Combine the chicken, cooled onions and peppers and spices in a medium-sized bowl. Mix well. Add egg and mix again. Add in heavy cream and mix well.

4. Heat a sauté pan over medium-high heat and add 2 Tablespoons olive oil. Drop heaping Tablespoons of the chicken mixture into the pan and cook the sausage patties for 2 minutes on each side, until they are browned and cooked through. Keep warm while you cook the remaining sausages and serve.

When you get tired of bacon, pork sausage or ham for breakfast, try these flavorful chicken sausage patties. They are very easy to prepare and offer a unique alternative to the usual breakfast meat. I prefer to use whole fennel seeds, lightly toasting them in the oven or in a small sauté pan, and grinding them in a spice grinder or mortar and pestle. Toasting the fennel intensifies the flavor and aroma of the spice and is well worth the extra effort. ∎

FRUIT FRITTERS

Firm fruits hold up better in these fritters, but almost any fruit will do. For breakfast I often choose a single fruit for the fritters and pair it with a complementing flavored crème anglaise. Here are some examples: Granny Smith apple fritters with a maple crème anglaise, summer berry fritters with a Chambord crème anglaise or banana fritters with a walnut crème anglaise. ∎

SERVES **8**

2 LARGE EGGS, SEPARATED
1/4 TEASPOON SALT
2 TABLESPOONS GRANULATED SUGAR
3/4 CUP WHOLE MILK
1 1/3 CUPS ALL-PURPOSE FLOUR
3–4 GRATES OF FRESH NUTMEG
3 CUPS CANOLA OIL FOR FRYING
2 1/2 CUPS FRUIT, CUT INTO UNIFORM 3/4-INCH PIECES (BERRIES, MELONS, BANANAS, APPLES, ETC.)
1/4 CUP POWDERED SUGAR, PLUS MORE FOR DUSTING
VANILLA CRÈME ANGLAISE (RECIPE FOLLOWS)

1. Whip the egg yolks for 30 seconds. Mix in the salt, sugar, milk, flour and nutmeg. Set this base aside for 1 hour.

2. Heat the oil in a large saucepan to 365 degrees (using a deep-fat thermometer).

3. Toss the fruit with powdered sugar to coat. Whip the egg whites to stiff peaks and fold into the base mixture with the fruit.

4. Drop heaping Tablespoonfuls of batter into the hot oil, and deep-fry for a little more than 2 minutes per side, or until golden. Drain on paper towels and sprinkle with powdered sugar.

5. Serve immediately on a pool of Vanilla crème anglaise.

RÈME ANGLAISE

2 CUPS WHOLE MILK
3 LARGE EGGS
2 EGG YOLKS
1/2 CUP GRANULATED SUGAR

1. Select the desired flavor from the list on the following page, making the required changes as noted.

2. Heat the milk in a 2-quart saucepan over medium-high heat and bring to a simmer.

3. In a medium-sized mixing bowl, whisk together the eggs, egg yolks and sugar. Have ready a large bowl half full of ice water (with plenty of ice) and a medium-sized bowl that will fit inside the ice bath. Also have on hand a fine mesh strainer, a wooden spoon and an instant read thermometer.

4. When the milk reaches a simmer, slowly pour about 1/2 cup of the hot milk into the egg mixture, whisking constantly. This is called tempering. Add another 1/2 cup of hot milk, whisking constantly. Now whisk the tempered egg mixture back into the saucepan with the milk, whisking constantly. Set the whisk aside and stir this mixture with the wooden spoon constantly over medium heat until the mixture reaches a temperature of 175 degrees on the instant read thermometer or until the mixture just coats the back of the spoon. Remove from the heat and immediately pour the mixture through the fine mesh strainer into the medium bowl. Immediately set this bowl in the ice bath to stop the cooking. Stir the mixture, occasionally, until it cools.

5. *Refrigerate in a covered container until needed, for up to 1 week.*

Crème anglaise is a versatile sauce that can be used with sweet breakfast dishes and desserts alike. Flavor it to coordinate with any dish by adding nuts, liqueurs, chocolate or spices. Crème anglaise is also a great base for ice cream. Simply pour the flavored crème anglaise into a prepared ice cream maker and you can create your favorite ice creams. ◾

VANILLA: Steep the milk with $1/2$ of a fresh vanilla bean, scraping out the seeds (or add 1 teaspoon of vanilla extract to the finished sauce)

GINGER: Steep the milk with 2 teaspoons freshly grated ginger

RASPBERRY: Add $1/2$ cup fresh or frozen raspberries and 1 Tablespoon Chambord after it cools

CHOCOLATE: Stir in $1/4$ cup chocolate syrup

ALMOND: Add 2 teaspoons crushed toasted almonds with 1 Tablespoon Amaretto

HAZELNUT: Add 2 teaspoons crushed hazelnuts with 1 Tablespoon Frangelico

PROSCIUTTO BAKED EGG WITH A SUN-DRIED TOMATO TORTILLA

SERVES 4

NONSTICK VEGETABLE SPRAY
$1/4$ POUND PROSCIUTTO HAM, THINLY SLICED
3 TABLESPOONS HEAVY CREAM
2 TABLESPOONS FINELY CHOPPED RED ONION
2 TABLESPOONS FINELY CHOPPED RED BELL PEPPER
8 LARGE EGGS
$1/2$ CUP SHREDDED SWISS CHEESE
1 SCALLION, GREEN PART ONLY, SLICED THIN
KOSHER SALT AND FRESHLY GROUND BLACK PEPPER
2 SUN-DRIED TOMATO FLOUR TORTILLAS (OR OTHER FLAVOR)
OLIVE OIL
FRUIT FOR GARNISH

Baking is an excellent way to prepare your morning eggs, especially if you are entertaining for breakfast, as I often do. Try this recipe with different meats, English muffins instead of the tortilla and hollandaise sauce. ■

1. Preheat the oven to 350 degrees and bring 2 cups of water to a boil in a teakettle or small saucepan. Take four 4-ounce (175 ml) clear pyrex bowls

Mary Jo came up with the name "Secret sauce" one day, when people kept asking about it and guessing the ingredients I used. It became kind of a game. I promised some guests the recipe would be included in this cookbook, so here it is. Mystery solved. ■

and spray them with nonstick vegetable spray. Line the inside of the bowls with the prosciutto. Divide the heavy cream between the bowls and sprinkle with half of the chopped red onion and red bell pepper. Crack two eggs into each bowl.

2. Place the bowls on a baking sheet with sides and place in the center of the preheated oven. Add enough boiling water (about a $^1\!/_4$ inch) to cover the bottom of the baking sheet. Bake for 30–40 minutes, or until the egg just sets up firmly. Don't overcook or the yolks will turn green.

3. Remove from the oven and divide the cheese between the bowls. Sprinkle with the scallions, salt and freshly ground black pepper. Return to the oven for 2 minutes, or until the cheese melts.

4. In a large sauté pan, heat $^1\!/_2$ teaspoon of the olive oil. Toast the tortilla lightly on each side and sprinkle with the kosher salt. Repeat with the other tortilla, oil and salt.

5. To serve, cut the tortillas in half. Roll the tortilla into a cone by taking one end and rolling it from the center of the long edge, following the curve of the tortilla.

6. Loosen the eggs from the bowl with a thin knife and lift from the bowls. Place the baked egg halfway in the tortilla cone and sprinkle with the remaining chopped red onion and red bell pepper. Garnish the plate with fresh fruit. This dish is great served with either a fresh hollandaise sauce or Michael's Secret sauce (recipe follows).

SECRET SAUCE

SERVES 4

1 CUP SOUR CREAM
1/2 CUP CHUNKY TOMATO SALSA (RECIPE IN SIDEBAR, PAGE 203)
    OR USE YOUR FAVORITE BRAND OF PREPARED SALSA
2 TABLESPOONS CHOPPED FRESH CILANTRO
1/4 TEASPOON KOSHER SALT
PINCH OF FRESHLY GROUND BLACK PEPPER

1. Simply mix all the ingredients together.

Baked Apple, Raisin and Cinnamon Pancakes

SERVES 6

2 1/4 CUPS ALL-PURPOSE FLOUR
1 TABLESPOON BAKING SODA
1 TEASPOON SALT
3 CUPS BUTTERMILK
3 LARGE EGGS, SEPARATED
8 TABLESPOONS UNSALTED BUTTER, MELTED
1 GRANNY SMITH APPLE
6 TABLESPOONS UNSALTED BUTTER
1/3 CUP REGULAR OR GOLDEN RAISINS
3/4 TEASPOON GROUND CINNAMON

1. Preheat the oven to 350 degrees.

2. Mix together the flour, baking soda and salt. Add the buttermilk and egg yolks

Baked pancakes are a great way to serve pancakes to a breakfast crowd. They can be prepared ahead, preferably as close to service as possible, and kept warm in the oven until serving time. These pancakes are hearty and will satisfy almost any appetite by themselves. Bananas can be substituted for the apples and nuts can be added if desired. ■

and mix well with a whisk. Add in the 8 Tablespoons of melted butter and stir until smooth.

3. Whip the egg whites in a mixer to medium peaks. Fold into batter.

4. Cut the apples in quarters, core and cut into small dice.

5. Nonstick 7-inch skillets are ideal for these pancakes. They must be ovenproof also, so if they have removable rubber handles, remove them. Heat the skillet over medium heat and add 1 Tablespoon of the butter and $\frac{1}{6}$ of the apple. Toss for a few minutes. Add $\frac{1}{6}$ of the raisins and $\frac{1}{6}$ of the cinnamon ($\frac{1}{8}$ teaspoon) and toss. Cook for 30 seconds. Pour in 1 heaping cup of the batter and stir briefly only to mix the apples and raisins into the batter. Cook over medium heat for about 3 minutes, or until pancake turns golden brown. Flip over with the assistance of a rubber spatula or an inverted plate and cook on the other side for 3 minutes, or until it is golden brown. Place the pancake on a baking sheet and finish making the other five pancakes in the same manner. If you use two or four pans, it goes that much quicker.

6. When all of the pancakes are made, place them in the oven for 7 minutes to finish cooking.

7. Sprinkle with powdered sugar and serve immediately with warmed maple syrup and the Cumin-spiced bacon and sausage roll (recipe follows).

CUMIN-SPICED BACON AND SAUSAGE ROLL

SERVES 4

FOUR 1-OUNCE PORK SAUSAGE BREAKFAST LINKS
4 SLICES OF "THICK SLICE" BACON (GET SPECIALTY SMOKED LIKE
    "APPLE-WOOD SMOKED," ETC.)
2 TEASPOONS CUMIN SPICE MIX (RECIPE BELOW)

1. Preheat the oven to 400 degrees.

2. Wrap each sausage link with one slice of bacon, overlapping as you move down the link, and secure with a toothpick.

3. Heat a small sauté pan over medium heat and sear the bacon and sausage rolls on all sides until the bacon is browned well. Roll in the Cumin spice mix, coating each lightly. Bake for 10 minutes, or until the sausage is cooked through.

CUMIN SPICE MIX

1/2 CUP LIGHT BROWN SUGAR, FIRMLY PACKED
2 TABLESPOONS CHILI POWDER
1 1/2 TEASPOONS GROUND CUMIN
2 TEASPOONS WHOLE CUMIN
1 TEASPOON GROUND CORIANDER
1/2 TEASPOON GROUND CARDAMOM
1/4 TEASPOON GROUND CINNAMON
1/4 TEASPOON GROUND CAYENNE PEPPER
2 TEASPOONS WHOLE ANISE SEEDS

1. Mix the sugar and spices together and store in an airtight container.

If you are looking for a unique breakfast meat, this is a nice alternative to strips of bacon or links of sausages on your breakfast plate. Thick-sliced bacon that has been smoked with specialty hard woods works the best, but any type will do. The spice mixture itself is quite versatile. It can be spread on plain bacon strips or sausage links as you finish cooking them, or for a distinctive taste, generously sprinkle over buttered squash as you bake it. ■

ATLANTIC SMOKED SALMON FRITTATA

SERVES 2

The frittatas I serve at the Inn are basically thick open-faced omelets. Toppings used are only limited by your imagination. Some of my favorite combinations include broccoli, bacon and Swiss cheese or bell peppers, prosciutto and Boursin cheese or cooked lobster, asparagus and Spanish Manchego cheese. Secret sauce (recipe, page 59) is a terrific accompaniment to these frittatas. ■

6 LARGE EGGS
1/4 CUP WHOLE MILK
1/4 TEASPOON KOSHER SALT
2 TABLESPOONS UNSALTED BUTTER
2 OUNCES ATLANTIC SMOKED SALMON
1/4 CUP GRATED SHARP VERMONT CHEDDAR
2 TABLESPOONS FINELY CHOPPED RED ONION
2 TABLESPOONS CAPERS
FRESHLY GROUND BLACK PEPPER
2 TABLESPOONS CHOPPED CHIVES
2 TABLESPOONS SOUR CREAM
FRUIT FOR GARNISH

1. These are individual open-faced frittatas. Crack the eggs in a medium-sized bowl. Whisk well. Add milk and salt, and mix.

2. In a 7-inch nonstick sauté pan, melt 1 Tablespoon of butter over medium heat. Add half of the egg mixture and stir gently (as you would for scrambled eggs) until the eggs are about 3/4 firm. Stop stirring and let the eggs set up. Flip over and firm up the other side. Remove to a baking sheet and cook the other half of the egg mixture in the same way.

3. Spread one ounce of the smoked salmon over each frittata. Evenly sprinkle the cheese, red onion and capers and crack some black pepper on each frittata.

4. Place the baking sheet under a salamander or broiler to melt the cheese and lightly brown the top of the frittatas. Sprinkle with the chives.

5. Serve with a spoonful of sour cream and a fruit garnish on the side.

LOBSTER AND ASPARAGUS QUICHE

SERVES 8–10

TWO 1½ POUND LIVE MAINE LOBSTERS (OR ¾ POUND
OF COOKED LOBSTER MEAT)
NONSTICK VEGETABLE SPRAY
1 BATCH PASTRY DOUGH (RECIPE, PAGE 67)
1 MEDIUM YELLOW ONION
1 POUND THIN ASPARAGUS
1 SMALL RED BELL PEPPER, FINELY CHOPPED
2 SCALLIONS, GREEN PART ONLY, SLICED
2 TABLESPOONS UNSALTED BUTTER
3 TEASPOONS KOSHER SALT, OR TO TASTE
1 TEASPOON FRESH OR DRIED THYME LEAVES, CRUMBLED
⅛ TEASPOON GROUND WHITE PEPPER
⅛ TEASPOON FRESHLY GRATED NUTMEG
8 OUNCES SWISS CHEESE, GRATED (ABOUT 2 CUPS)
9 LARGE EGGS
1 CUP WHOLE MILK

Gourmet magazine featured this recipe in its May 1999 issue. Maine lobster is abundant in Camden, but it may be too expensive and difficult to find in your part of the country. Crabmeat, shrimp, ham or even other vegetables can be substituted for the ¾ pound of cooked lobster meat. ■

1. Skip this first part if you are using precooked lobster meat. For the lobsters, fill a large (9-quart or larger) stockpot with 2 inches of water, cover and bring to a boil. Add live lobsters, cover and cook for 10 minutes. Remove from the water and let cool. When cool, crack lobsters and remove the meat from the claws, knuckles and tails (discarding the vein). Discard shells and reserve the lobster meat.

2. Spray a 9-inch scalloped tart pan (with removable bottom and 2-inch sides) with vegetable spray. Lightly flour dough and roll out into a 12-inch circle (about ⅛-inch thick). Invert dough onto tart pan and form dough into the

pan, evenly distributing the dough to form a $^1/_8$-inch crust across the bottom and up the sides. Remove excess dough for another use. With a fork, prick the dough all over. Chill, covered with plastic wrap, until firm, about 30 minutes, and up to 1 day.

3. Preheat the oven to 350 degrees.

4. Finely chop the onion. Prepare the asparagus by removing the tough white bottoms and peeling the bottom 2 inches of the stalks if they feel tough. Cut into $^1/_2$-inch pieces. Cut enough red bell pepper (small dice) to measure $^1/_2$ cup. Thinly slice the scallions. In a large nonstick skillet, cook onion in butter over moderate heat, stirring until softened. Add asparagus and stir, cooking 3 minutes. Remove skillet from heat and stir in chopped red bell pepper, scallion, salt, thyme, white pepper and nutmeg. Cool mixture. *Vegetable mixture may be made 1 day ahead and chilled, covered.*

Maine Lobsters from Captain Andy

LIKE A TRUE Maine lobsterman, Arthur Andrews sees little romance in what he does. His boat *The Whistler* was named by the man who sold it to him. He attributes the fact that customers flock to Captain Andy's—his lobster shack on Washington Street in Camden—to the advertisements he places in local publications rather than any native superiority in his clams and lobsters. And as for any changes in the lobstering business during the 40 years he's been at it, Andrews says the only significant one is more reporting to regulators about what goes on at the shack.

Andrews is a native of Whiting, a tiny Downeast town that had a two-room schoolhouse until 1997. Since the early 1960s, he's gone lobstering every single day, even when it meant spending hours on the ocean before his day job as an educator began. These days, he tends his pots in the waters of Camden and the nearby islands in Penobscot Bay. He does the fishing and his wife Marlene runs the business at Captain Andy's, where you can't get a lobster roll or fried clams, but you can buy lobster and clams one of two ways—live or cooked.

5. Line the dough shell with parchment paper and fill with pie weights or raw dry beans. Bake shell in the middle of the oven until sides are firm enough to hold their shape, 15 to 20 minutes, and carefully remove parchment paper and weights or beans.

6. Cut lobster into 1/2-inch pieces. Add lobster and cheese to the vegetable mixture, stirring to combine, and spoon mixture into the shell. In a bowl, whisk together the eggs and the milk.

7. Place the tart pan on a baking sheet, pour the egg mixture into the shell and bake quiche in the middle of the oven until filling is set and a tester comes out clean, about 90 minutes.

8. Cool quiche in pan on a rack for 15 minutes before cutting it into 8 or 10 wedges. The quiche cuts easier once it has cooled. *The quiche can be prepared days in advance, and individual slices can be heated in the microwave.*

PASTRY DOUGH

> 1 1/3 CUPS ALL-PURPOSE FLOUR
> 3/4 TEASPOON KOSHER SALT
> 1/2 STICK (4 TABLESPOONS) CHILLED, UNSALTED BUTTER
> 1/3 CUP VEGETABLE SHORTENING
> 1/4 CUP COLD WATER

1. In a mixer, combine the flour and salt. Cut the butter into fine cubes and mix into the flour until it resembles a fine meal. Add the shortening and mix for 30 seconds. Add the water and mix only until it combines. Do not overwork. Remove from the mixer and wrap in plastic wrap.

2. Refrigerate for at least 2 hours.

This pastry dough is a terrific recipe and can be used on tarts and pies. As always is the case with pie dough, don't overwork the dough. The more you work it, the tougher it gets.

H

Afternoon Tea and Cookies

AFTERNOON TEA, which is served from 3 p.m. to 5 p.m., is the highlight of what Mary Jo calls a "special time of the day" at the Hartstone Inn. As new guests check in, those who have been at the Inn for a day or two wander in from shopping in Camden, hiking Mt. Battie or exploring more of Maine's beautiful mid-coast region. The atmosphere is relaxed and friendly.

In the library, guests help themselves to Pickwick Teas imported from Holland—just try to read the Dutch on the packages—and a selection of freshly baked cookies. As you'd expect from innkeepers who pay attention to every detail, the baked goods are both homemade and irresistibly delicious. There's something for every sweet tooth, from Lemon-poppy seed bread or Ruthie's chocolate Chambord cookies to biscotti or old-fashioned chocolate chip cookies.

Guests are welcome to take their tea and cookies to their rooms for a little hibernating. They can also pull up a chair in the library for a game of chess or relax on a sofa in the parlor to read a magazine. Or, guests can explore the third-floor game room, where cards and board games are available for their enjoyment.

BUTTER COOKIES

MAKES 24 COOKIES

1 CUP UNSALTED BUTTER, SOFTENED
2/3 CUP GRANULATED SUGAR
2 EGG YOLKS
2 TEASPOONS VANILLA EXTRACT
2 1/2 CUPS ALL-PURPOSE FLOUR
JELLY, JAM OR PRESERVES OF YOUR CHOICE

1. Preheat the oven to 350 degrees.

2. Cream together the butter and sugar. Mix in the egg yolks and vanilla, followed by the flour, mixing well until a ball forms.

3. Roll into small balls (we use a #40 ice cream scoop to portion cookies) and press thumb into center. Place about 1 inch apart on a baking sheet lined with a nonstick baking mat or on a lightly greased baking sheet.

4. Fill center with any flavor jelly, jam or preserves.

5. Bake for 15–18 minutes or until lightly browned around the bottom. Transfer the cookies to cooling racks to cool.

These butter cookies, also referred to as "thumb prints," are similar in taste and texture to shortbread cookies and can be filled with your favorite jam, jelly or preserves. For a chocolate butter cookie, add another 1/4 cup of flour in step 2 and drizzle in 1/2 cup of melted dark chocolate at the end of step 2.

Ginger Snaps

MAKES 35 COOKIES

1/2 CUP UNSALTED BUTTER, SOFTENED
1/2 CUP VEGETABLE SHORTENING
1/2 CUP GRANULATED SUGAR
1/2 CUP DARK BROWN SUGAR, FIRMLY PACKED
1 LARGE EGG
1/2 CUP MOLASSES
2 TABLESPOONS FINELY GRATED PEELED GINGERROOT
2 TEASPOONS FRESHLY GRATED ORANGE ZEST
2 1/2 CUPS ALL-PURPOSE FLOUR
2 TEASPOONS BAKING SODA
2 TEASPOONS GROUND GINGER
2 TEASPOONS GROUND CINNAMON
1 TEASPOON GROUND CLOVES
1/2 TEASPOON SALT
1/4 CUP CRYSTALLIZED GINGER, ROUGHLY CUT
ADDITIONAL GRANULATED SUGAR FOR COATING

1. Preheat the oven to 350 degrees.

2. In mixer, beat together the butter, shortening and sugars. Add the egg and molasses and mix well. Add the fresh grated ginger and orange zest and mix to combine. In another bowl, combine the flour, baking soda, ground ginger, cinnamon, cloves and salt. Add dry ingredients to mixer. Mix until combined. Add the crystallized ginger and combine.

3. Roll the dough into walnut-sized balls (we use a #40 ice cream scoop to portion cookies) and roll the balls in granulated sugar. Bake as balls (do not press

Ginger snaps are one of my personal favorite cookies. I use fresh, ground and crystallized ginger along with lots of spices to create a very flavorful cookie. The grated orange zest adds just the right amount of citrus bitterness to the recipe. If you plan on freezing some or all of the cookie dough, omit the part in step 3 about rolling the dough in granulated sugar until you are ready for baking.

down). Place about 2 inches apart on a baking sheet lined with a nonstick baking mat or on a lightly greased baking sheet.

4. Bake for 20–22 minutes, until golden and the tops start to crack. Transfer the cookies to cooling racks to cool.

Butterscotch Chip Oatmeal Cookies

MAKES 45 COOKIES

1 CUP UNSALTED BUTTER, SOFTENED
1/2 CUP BROWN SUGAR, FIRMLY PACKED
1/2 CUP GRANULATED SUGAR
2 LARGE EGGS
1 TEASPOON VANILLA EXTRACT
2 TABLESPOONS WATER
2 CUPS ALL-PURPOSE FLOUR
1/2 TEASPOON BAKING POWDER
1 TEASPOON SALT
1 CUP SHREDDED COCONUT
1 CUP PECAN PIECES
2 CUPS OLD-FASHIONED ROLLED OATS
1 1/2 CUPS BUTTERSCOTCH CHIPS

1. In a bowl with an electric mixer, cream the butter. Add the sugars and beat until mixture is light and fluffy. Beat in the eggs, vanilla extract and 2 Tablespoons of water.

2. In another bowl, whisk together the flour, baking powder, and salt. Add the flour mixture to the butter mixture gradually, and beat until it is just combined.

The ingredients in this recipe yield some impressive cookies. Butterscotch chips, oatmeal, coconut and pecans— how can you go wrong? At the Inn, we use nonstick baking mats to line the bottom of our baking pans when baking cookies. Various brands are available on the market today and they make removal of the cookies and cleanup a cinch. They are well worth the investment. ■

3. Gently stir in the coconut, pecan pieces, oats and butterscotch chips.

4. Make balls with a #40 ice cream scoop and place 2 inches apart on baking sheets lined with a nonstick baking mat or on lightly greased baking sheets.

5. Bake for 15 minutes. Transfer the cookies to cooling racks to cool.

CRANBERRY AND WHITE CHOCOLATE CHUNK COOKIES

MAKES 25 COOKIES

1/2 CUP GRANULATED SUGAR
1/2 CUP VEGETABLE SHORTENING
2 LARGE EGGS
1 TEASPOON VANILLA EXTRACT
1 CUP ALL-PURPOSE FLOUR
1 CUP QUICK COOKING OATS
1 TEASPOON BAKING POWDER
1 CUP WHITE CHOCOLATE CHUNKS (PEA SIZE)
1/2 CUP DRIED CRANBERRIES
1/2 CUP SHREDDED COCONUT
1/2 CUP CASHEW HALVES

1. Preheat the oven to 350 degrees.

2. In a mixer, combine the sugar, shortening, eggs and vanilla. Add the flour, oats and baking powder and mix until well combined. Gently stir in the white chocolate, cranberries, coconut and cashews by hand.

3. Make balls with a #40 ice cream scoop and place about 2 inches apart on a baking sheet lined with a nonstick baking mat or on a lightly greased baking sheet. Pat down the balls to make 3/4-inch disks.

We make full batches of cookies and form them into consistent-sized balls with a #40 ice cream scoop onto a baking sheet lined with parchment paper. We then freeze the balls of dough on the cookie sheet (it usually takes about 2 hours) and then we transfer the balls of dough into freezer bags and place in the freezer until needed. Since the balls were frozen individually first, it is easy to remove the number of cookies needed at any given time. Thaw, bake and they're ready to eat.

4. Bake for 10–12 minutes, just until they begin to brown along the bottom edge. Transfer the cookies to cooling racks to cool.

CHOCOLATE CHIP AND WALNUT COOKIES

MAKES 40 COOKIES

1 CUP VEGETABLE SHORTENING
1 CUP GRANULATED SUGAR
1/2 CUP BROWN SUGAR, FIRMLY PACKED
2 LARGE EGGS
2 TEASPOONS VANILLA EXTRACT
2 CUPS ALL-PURPOSE FLOUR
1 TEASPOON BAKING SODA
1 1/2 TEASPOONS SALT
2 CUPS CHOCOLATE CHIPS
1 CUP WALNUT PIECES

1. Preheat the oven to 350 degrees.

2. Cream together the shortening, sugars, eggs and vanilla until fluffy.

3. Mix together the flour, baking soda and salt. Stir into creamed mixture. Mix in the chocolate chips and walnut pieces by hand.

4. Make balls with a #40 ice cream scoop and place about 2 inches apart on a baking sheet lined with a nonstick baking mat or on a lightly greased baking sheet.

5. Bake for 15 minutes. Transfer the cookies to cooling racks to cool.

We serve many different cookies at the Inn during Afternoon Tea. Guests frequently request various cookie recipes and this familiar cookie always receives its fair share of requests. These chocolate chip cookies can be made without the walnuts if desired, or another type of chopped nut can easily be substituted. If you really like chocolate, add 2 Tablespoons cocoa powder and 2 Tablespoons chocolate syrup to the recipe, and replace the chocolate chips with an equivalent amount of 1/2-inch dark chocolate chunks. ▪

Peanut Butter Cookies

MAKES 35 COOKIES

1 CUP VEGETABLE SHORTENING
1 CUP GRANULATED SUGAR
1 CUP BROWN SUGAR, FIRMLY PACKED
1 TEASPOON SALT
2 LARGE EGGS
1 CUP CHUNKY PEANUT BUTTER
2½ CUPS ALL-PURPOSE FLOUR
1 TEASPOON BAKING SODA
ADDITIONAL GRANULATED SUGAR (COARSE BAKING SUGAR,
    IF AVAILABLE) FOR DECORATING

I have fond memories of my mother's peanut butter cookies. She'd dip her fork in water and sugar to etch the cookies with a crisscross pattern. Then she usually topped the cookies with a large chocolate Hershey's kiss. Wow, those were good. At the Inn, we use chunky peanut butter to give the cookies a little extra texture. To yield a cookie with even more crunch, add more coarsely chopped peanuts. ∎

1. Preheat the oven to 350 degrees.

2. Cream together the shortening, sugars, salt and eggs. Add peanut butter and mix well.

3. Sift together the flour and baking soda; stir into the creamed mixture.

4. Make balls with a #40 ice cream scoop and place about 2 inches apart on a baking sheet lined with a nonstick baking mat or on a lightly greased baking sheet. Press down with the tines of a large fork in a crisscross pattern and sprinkle the top with coarse baking sugar.

5. Bake for 15 minutes. Transfer the cookies to cooling racks to cool.

Dried Fruit and Oatmeal Cookies

MAKES 40 COOKIES

1 CUP UNSALTED BUTTER, SOFTENED

1/2 CUP GRANULATED SUGAR

1 CUP BROWN SUGAR, FIRMLY PACKED

2 LARGE EGGS

1 TEASPOON VANILLA EXTRACT

1 TEASPOON LEMON EXTRACT

1 1/2 CUPS ALL-PURPOSE FLOUR

1 TEASPOON BAKING SODA

1 TEASPOON GROUND CINNAMON

3 CUPS OLD-FASHIONED OATS

1/2 CUP GOLDEN RAISINS

1/4 CUP DRIED CURRANTS

3/4 CUP VARIOUS DRIED FRUITS (MANGO, DATES, FIGS,
CRANBERRIES, ETC.), CHOPPED TO THE SIZE OF RAISINS

1. Preheat the oven to 350 degrees.

2. In a mixer, cream together the butter and sugars. Add the eggs, vanilla and lemon extract and mix.

3. In another bowl, combine the flour, baking soda and cinnamon. Add to the sugar and egg mixture and combine. Add the oats, raisins, currants and dried fruits and gently mix in by hand.

4. Make balls with a #40 ice cream scoop and place about 2 inches apart on a baking sheet lined with a nonstick baking mat or on a lightly greased baking sheet.

5. Bake for 12–15 minutes. Transfer the cookies to cooling racks to cool.

There's something about the flavor and texture that dried fruits give to cookies. I love it. A combination of dried fruits can be used, or you may prefer to create a single fruit cookie such as Dried "Mango" and Oatmeal Cookies.

Ruthie made these wonderful cookies one day and we immediately added them to our list of regular tea offerings. Ruthie and her husband Josh are our invaluable assistants at the Inn, and one of the many things that Ruthie takes care of is the baking of cookies and pastries for our Afternoon Tea. If you are planning to freeze some of the dough balls for later use, omit rolling in the powdered sugar until you are ready to bake them. ■

Ruthie's Chocolate-Chambord Cookies

MAKES 30 COOKIES

1/2 CUP CANOLA OIL

4 OUNCES UNSWEETENED CHOCOLATE, MELTED

2 CUPS GRANULATED SUGAR

4 LARGE EGGS

2 TABLESPOONS CHAMBORD LIQUEUR

2 CUPS ALL-PURPOSE FLOUR

2 TEASPOONS BAKING POWDER

1/2 TEASPOON SALT

1/2 CUP COARSELY CHOPPED DARK CHOCOLATE

POWDERED SUGAR FOR COATING

1. Preheat the oven to 350 degrees.

2. In a mixer, cream together the oil, melted chocolate and sugar. Add the eggs and Chambord and mix.

3. In another bowl, combine the flour, baking powder and salt. Add to the sugar and egg mixture and combine. Add the chocolate chunks and gently mix in by hand. Chill for at least 3 hours to make it easy to scoop.

4. Make balls with a #40 ice cream scoop and roll them in powdered sugar and coat well. Place about 2 inches apart on a baking sheet lined with a nonstick baking mat or on a lightly greased baking sheet.

5. Bake for 20 minutes. Transfer the cookies to cooling racks to cool.

ISA'S ALMOND AND APRICOT BISCOTTI

MAKES 40 COOKIES

2 3/4 CUPS ALL-PURPOSE FLOUR
1 1/2 CUPS GRANULATED SUGAR
2 1/2 TEASPOONS BAKING POWDER
1 TEASPOON SALT
1 TEASPOON GROUND GINGER
1/2 CUP UNSALTED BUTTER, CHILLED AND CUT INTO SMALL PIECES
2 LARGE EGGS
1/4 CUP, PLUS 1 TABLESPOON GRAND MARNIER OR
    APRICOT BRANDY
2 TEASPOONS ALMOND EXTRACT
4 OUNCES WHITE CHOCOLATE, MEDIUM-COARSE CHOP
1 2/3 CUPS WHOLE ALMONDS, TOASTED AND COARSELY CHOPPED
6 OUNCES DRIED APRICOTS, CUT INTO A SMALL DICE

1. Line a baking sheet with a nonstick baking mat or a piece of foil that has been buttered and floured.

2. Combine the flour, sugar, baking powder, salt and ginger in the bowl of a food processor. Pulse a few times to combine the ingredients. Add the butter and process until a fine meal forms.

3. In a large bowl, beat the eggs, Grand Marnier (or brandy) and almond extract. Add the flour mixture, white chocolate, almonds and apricots to the eggs and stir until a moist dough forms.

4. Divide the dough in thirds and form into three logs on the prepared sheet, spacing them evenly. Moisten fingertips and shape each dough log into a

Lisa and her husband Paul have come to visit us every year from the Chicago area and have become great friends. Lisa is a very talented artist and has faux painted numerous guest rooms while Paul knows about all there is to know about wine and has done some consulting work on our wine list. Every Christmas, Lisa sends me a box of these wonderful biscotti she makes they don't last long!

3-inch wide by 10-inch long rectangular strip. Cover with plastic wrap and refrigerate for 30 minutes, or until the dough is firm.

5. Position the rack in the center of the oven and preheat to 350 degrees.

6. Bake until the logs are golden brown, about 30 minutes. Transfer sheet to a rack and cool completely. Reduce oven temperature to 300 degrees.

7. Remove logs from the sheet and transfer to a cutting board. Using a serrated knife, carefully cut each log crosswise into ³/₄-inch wide slices. Arrange the cookies, cut side down, on two baking sheets with parchment paper. Bake for 10 minutes. Gently turn the cookies over and bake 10 minutes longer. Transfer cookies to cooling racks and cool completely. *Biscotti keep well for 2–3 weeks if stored in an airtight container at room temperature. They also freeze well.*

MAPLE SCONES

MAKES 8 LARGE SCONES

3 CUPS ALL-PURPOSE FLOUR

1 TABLESPOON BAKING POWDER

¹/₂ TEASPOON SALT

¹/₄ CUP GRANULATED SUGAR

¹/₄ CUP BROWN SUGAR, FIRMLY PACKED

¹/₂ CUP UNSALTED BUTTER, CHILLED

¹/₄ CUP PURE MAPLE SYRUP

1 CUP HEAVY CREAM

3 EGG YOLKS

2 TEASPOONS MAPLE EXTRACT

¹/₂ CUP PECAN PIECES

1 LARGE EGG

1 TEASPOON WATER

Scones are one of my favorite tea accompaniments and this particular recipe creates a scone that's not too sweet. The state of Maine produces some terrific maple syrup, which gives a wonderful balance to this recipe. To make blueberry scones, leave out the maple syrup and the maple extract and add 1 cup fresh or frozen blueberries and 2 teaspoons vanilla extract. For chocolate chip scones, add ¹/₄ cup chocolate syrup and 1 cup miniature chocolate chips to the recipe, omitting the maple syrup and maple extract.

1. Preheat the oven to 400 degrees.

2. Line a baking sheet with a nonstick baking mat or parchment paper.

3. Mix flour, baking powder, salt and sugars together in a large bowl. Dice the chilled butter and work it into the flour mixture with your fingertips until the mixture resembles coarse meal.

4. In another bowl, whisk together the maple syrup, heavy cream, egg yolks, maple extract and pecan pieces. Add the wet mixture to the dry mixture and stir to combine. Turn dough out onto a counter and knead gently for 1 minute.

5. Roll the dough out into an 8-inch round, and cut the dough into 8 wedges. Transfer the wedges to the lined baking sheet, spacing them about 2 inches apart.

6. In a small bowl, whisk together the egg and 1 teaspoon of water. Brush each scone with the glaze.

7. Bake in the center of the preheated oven for about 20 minutes, until they are lightly browned. Cool slightly and serve warmed or at room temperature.

H

Dinner at Seven

DINNER AT SEVEN

ONCE OUR Inn guests have been treated to one of our sumptuous breakfasts, it seems they realize what a splendid opportunity they have to experience the real thing—dinner at the Hartstone Inn—and they request reservations.

An evening meal at the Inn consists of a five-course prix-fixe menu, which changes daily. The menu is shaped by a number of factors, including the seasonality and availability of food products, guest allergies or dislikes (we note these when we take reservations) and the past history of the guests who are dining with us that evening. We keep a record of our return dinner guests and the menu items they were served on each visit to our dining room. Before my morning trip to the market, I consult this record to rule out dishes any guest would have been served in the recent past.

A candlelit gourmet dinner in the Hartstone Inn dining room is an intimate experience. With only seven tables and a maximum of twenty guests, one need not worry about cramped dining or slow service. Since the only menu choices to make are from the wine and beverage list, diners will be enjoying their first course shortly after receiving their drinks. We have a few regular guests who prefer not to see that night's menu so they may treat each course as a surprise.

Intense flavors are best served in an appetizer portion, which is one of the reasons I love making appetizers. They simply afford me the best opportunity to create and combine a wide mix of flavors and ethnic influences. Menus may begin with homemade lobster raviolis, Thai crab spring rolls or Jerk-seared tuna with fresh mango. From late fall into early spring, what follows next is usually a uniquely seasonal soup. As soon as the first greens of spring arrive, however, fresh salads adorn the tables, most often dressed with a fresh fruit dressing and local produce. Our intermezzo course is sorbet, ranging from wild Maine blueberry to summer peach.

Entrées at the Inn often incorporate locally caught fish and shellfish, which are abundant year-round in our seaside community. Local "diver" scallops, hand harvested from the St. Georges River, farm-raised Atlantic salmon, Gulf of Maine haddock and, of course, our succulent Maine lobster are just a few of the specialties from the sea that might end up elegantly presented on your plate. Other evenings, entrées may feature olive-encrusted rack of lamb, Cajun-seared filet mignon or pan-seared duck breast with herbes de Provence.

To end a gourmet five-course meal with any ordinary dessert is criminal. Ask anyone who has dined with us about his or her meal, and I can almost guarantee a reference to our dessert soufflés, a signature dish at the Hartstone Inn. Occasionally I will slip in a crème brûlée or the Pistachio-chocolate ganache tart, but I will invariably get a response like "No soufflés tonight? I've heard so much about them and was so looking forward to enjoying one."

Appetizers

CARIBBEAN TENDERLOIN OF PORK WITH A MANGO-CILANTRO SALSA

SERVES 4

1 WHOLE PORK TENDERLOIN (ABOUT 1¼ POUNDS)
2 TABLESPOONS OLIVE OIL
1 TABLESPOON CARIBBEAN DRY SPICE MIX (RECIPE, PAGE 169)
½ TEASPOON KOSHER SALT
LIME SLICES, RED BELL PEPPER DIAMONDS AND CILANTRO SPRIGS
    FOR GARNISH
1 BATCH OF MANGO-CILANTRO SALSA (RECIPE BELOW)

1. Remove the fat and silver skin from the pork tenderloin.

2. Coat the pork with olive oil and sprinkle with the Caribbean dry spice mix and kosher salt. Let marinate for at least 2 hours in the refrigerator.

MANGO-CILANTRO SALSA

1 RIPE MANGO, CUT INTO ¼-INCH CUBES
2 TABLESPOONS FINELY CHOPPED RED ONION
2 TABLESPOONS FINELY CHOPPED GREEN BELL PEPPER
2 TABLESPOONS FINELY CHOPPED RED BELL PEPPER
⅛ HABANERO CHILI, MINCED (MORE IF YOU LIKE IT HOT)
1 TABLESPOON CHOPPED CILANTRO
½ LIME, JUICED
KOSHER SALT AND WHITE PEPPER TO TASTE

1. To make the mango salsa, combine all ingredients and mix well. Reserve.

2. Preheat the oven to 350 degrees.

Pork is the perfect meat to match up with my Caribbean dry spice mix. In the warmer months I often coat a whole pork tenderloin with canola oil, salt and Caribbean dry spice mix, marinate it for 2 hours and grill it on a hot barbecue grill. The mango-cilantro salsa is the ideal "cool" accompaniment for the spicy pork. To create the red pepper diamonds I refer to in this recipe, slice ⅜ inch strips of red bell peppers, and cut each strip on an angle in about ½-inch pieces. ∎

The term timbale in

culinary terms refers to a

cylindrical form of food,

creatively formed and usually

stacked inside a round mold.

For my summer vegetable

timbale, I went to the

hardware store and purchased

some PVC pipe that has a

3-inch inside diameter, and

cut it into 3-inch sections.

Stainless steel timbale rings of

all sizes are also available at

cooking supply stores if your

budget permits. ■

3. Heat a large sauté or grill pan over high heat. Place the pork tenderloin in the hot pan and sear, sealing in the juices. Turn every 20 seconds or so, browning all sides. Transfer the pork to an ovenproof pan and roast in the oven for about 35–40 minutes.

4. Remove from the oven and let the pork rest for 5 minutes.

5. To serve, garnish each plate with a lime slice, red bell pepper diamonds and cilantro sprigs. Place a spoonful of salsa on the plate and slice the pork into $3/8$-inch slices on the bias.

6. Divide the pork between the four plates, fanning it out. Serve.

GRILLED SUMMER VEGETABLE TIMBALE WITH GOAT CHEESE AND BASIL

SERVES 4

2 BEETS
1 MEDIUM ZUCCHINI
1 MEDIUM YELLOW SQUASH
2 MEDIUM-SIZED CARROTS
1 PORTABELLA MUSHROOM
1 MEDIUM BEEFSTEAK TOMATO
12 SPEARS ASPARAGUS (PENCIL SIZE)
EXTRA VIRGIN OLIVE OIL
KOSHER SALT AND FRESHLY GROUND BLACK PEPPER
1 TEASPOON CHOPPED FRESH BASIL
2 TABLESPOONS BALSAMIC VINEGAR
6 CHERRY TOMATOES
3 OUNCES FRESH GOAT CHEESE
4 SPRIGS FRESH BASIL, FOR GARNISH

1. Boil the beets until fork tender. Remove skin and cool. Slice each into 4 slices.

2. Remove ends and slice both the zucchini and yellow squash into 8 equal slices on a slight bias. Peel carrots and cut into sticks 2 inches long and $^1/_2$ inch by $^1/_2$ inch. Core the tomato and slice into 4 equal slices. Clean the portabella mushroom and cut into 8 wedges. Cut the tough part (pale color) off the bottom of the asparagus spears and peel the lower half of the spears, removing the tougher outside shell.

3. Blanch the carrot slices in boiling water for 2 minutes to partially cook them and cool them off in a bowl of ice water. Lay all of the vegetables out on a baking sheet (use one with sides) and drizzle with the olive oil. Sprinkle with the kosher salt and freshly ground black pepper. Turn them over and coat the other side. Let sit for 15 minutes.

4. Using either a stove top grill pan or a barbecue grill, grill the vegetables (reserving the marinating oil and juices) on each side, just enough to mark them and cook them slightly. The tomatoes cook very quickly. Do not overcook any of the vegetables. Remove from the grill to another baking sheet.

5. To make the vinaigrette, mix the chopped basil with the balsamic vinegar. Place in a small container with a lid. In a $^1/_4$-cup measurer, pour in the reserved oil and juices, and fill the remaining way with additional olive oil. Add to the container a few grinds of pepper and a pinch of salt. Cover and shake gently.

6. For assembly and presentation, place a 3-inch timbale mold (I use a 3-inch piece of PVC pipe that has a 3-inch inside diameter) on the center of a 12-inch dinner plate. Layer in the vegetables in this order: 1 tomato slice, 2 zucchini slices, 2 beet slices, 2 yellow squash slices, 6 carrot sticks, and 2 mushroom wedges. Build each layer securely on top of each other and press down gently on the vegetables to firm up the stack. Remove the mold form. Decorate the plate with the 3 asparagus spears, 3 cherry tomato halves, and a

Appleton Creamery's
Goat Cheese

WHEN CAITLIN HUNTER says Appleton Creamery is a family business, she's not kidding. She is the focal point of the family's goat cheese business, designing and producing the cheeses, milking the goats and handling distribution at farmers' markets throughout Maine. Husband Bradley, who is also a sail maker, built the workrooms where Caitlin makes the cheese and the barn that houses more than 50 American Alpine goats. And daughter Fiona, 14, makes goat-milk fudge and is her mother's girl Friday at the markets, where the crowd is frequently three-deep at the Appleton Creamery table.

The draw for all those hungry shoppers is Caitlin's award-winning chevre. You can buy it three ways: wrapped in grape leaves, rolled in black peppercorns or marinated in olive oil with garlic and herbs. Caitlin's original plan, hatched when the Hunters got their state license to produce goat cheese in 1994, was to use the chevre to barter for chicken, beef and the few vegetables the family doesn't grow in their organic garden. Nowadays though, Appleton Creamery does much more than feed the Hunter family. Michael, one of the countless Appleton Creamery fans in the state, uses it for his Grilled Summer Vegetable Timbale.

sprig of fresh basil. Slice the goat cheese and arrange around the plate. Drizzle with vinaigrette and serve.

MAINE LOBSTER AND VEGETABLE TIMBALE WITH A COCONUT CURRY SAUCE

SERVES 4

TWO 1½ POUND LIVE MAINE LOBSTERS
½ POUND CARROTS
1 POUND SNOW PEAS
2 RED BELL PEPPERS
3 TABLESPOONS UNSALTED BUTTER
KOSHER SALT AND FRESHLY GROUND BLACK PEPPER
COCONUT CURRY SAUCE (RECIPE FOLLOWS)
2 SCALLIONS, GREEN PART ONLY, SLICED THINLY ON THE BIAS

1. Fill a large 9-quart stockpot with two inches of water; cover and bring to a boil. Add live lobsters, cover and cook for 10 minutes. Remove from the water and let cool. When cool, crack lobsters and remove the meat from the claws, knuckles and tails (discarding the vein). Reserve the tail fin for garnish and discard the remaining shells.

2. Slice the lobster tails in half lengthwise and place all of the lobster meat and the tail fins on a buttered ovenproof pan or plate with sides just large enough to hold the meat in a single layer. Brush the lobster with a thin coating of the Coconut curry sauce. Cover with foil. Reserve.

3. Bring 1 quart of water to a boil in a medium-sized saucepan. Peel the carrots and remove the ends. Slice on the bias into ⅛-inch medallions. Snap the ends off the snow peas and pull away the strings. When the water boils, add 1 Tablespoon

Vegetables of your choice can be substituted for the carrots and snow peas in this recipe. Blanch the vegetables so they are cooked but still retain their crispness. If live Maine lobsters are not available in your area or are out of your price range, large shrimp would be a good substitute. Overcooked shellfish becomes tough, so regardless of whether you are using lobster or shrimp, cook only until it is just done. ■

salt and the carrots. Blanch for 2 minutes. Remove immediately to an ice bath to cool. Bring the water back to a boil and blanch the snow peas for 20 seconds. Remove immediately to an ice bath to cool. When thoroughly cooled, remove the carrots and snow peas from the ice water and drain off excess water. Lay the vegetables out on a buttered baking sheet (with sides). Brush with 2 Tablespoons melted butter and season with kosher salt and freshly ground black pepper.

4. Burn the skin of the bell peppers over an open flame and place in a plastic bag to steam for 3 minutes. Peel away the charred skin. Cut each in half and remove the seeds and stem. Cut each into 8 strips. Place on the baking sheet with the carrots and snow peas and season with salt and pepper.

5. Heat the oven to 350 degrees. Place the tray of vegetables and the lobster (in prepared pans) in the oven for 10 minutes. Place a 3-inch timbale mold (I use a 3-inch piece of PVC pipe that has a 3-inch inside diameter) on each serving plate. Layer the vegetables and lobster alternately inside the timbale molds, building each layer securely on top of each other. Press down gently on the lobster and vegetables. Ladle a small amount of the Coconut curry sauce (the sauce is rich) around the timbale and remove the ring. Garnish with the reserved fin tail and sliced scallions.

Coconut Curry Sauce

1/3 cup Coco Lopez (sweetened coconut cream)
1/4 cup fresh lime juice
2 tablespoons minced scallions, green part only
1 teaspoon curry powder
1/4 teaspoon cayenne pepper
1/4 teaspoon salt

1. Whisk together the Coco Lopez and the lime juice until blended.

2. Add the minced scallions, curry powder, cayenne pepper and salt; mix well.

My coconut curry sauce is quite rich, so use it sparingly — a little of this sauce goes a long way. The sweetness of the coconut cream, the heat from the cayenne pepper and the tartness from the lime combine with the curry powder to create a unique and flavorful sauce.

Duck Breast and Portabella Mushroom Tartlet with herbes de Provence

SERVES 4

2 DUCK BREASTS, EXCESS FAT AND TENDONS TRIMMED
1 TABLESPOON OLIVE OIL
2 LARGE PINCHES KOSHER SALT
1 TEASPOON HERBES DE PROVENCE
1 BATCH PASTRY DOUGH (RECIPE, PAGE 67)

MUSHROOMS

3 TABLESPOONS OLIVE OIL
2 LARGE PORTABELLA MUSHROOMS
1 CUP FINELY CHOPPED YELLOW ONION
2 CLOVES GARLIC, MINCED
KOSHER SALT AND WHITE PEPPER TO TASTE
3 TABLESPOONS DRY SHERRY
1/2 CUP HEAVY CREAM
4 TABLESPOONS UNSALTED BUTTER, SOFT
SALT AND WHITE PEPPER TO TASTE
4 TEASPOONS GRATED PARMESAN CHEESE
1 PLUM TOMATO, SEEDED AND CUT INTO LONG STRIPS, FOR GARNISH
1 TEASPOON CHOPPED CHIVES, FOR GARNISH

1. Coat the duck breasts with olive oil and season with kosher salt and the herbes de Provence. Set in the refrigerator to marinate until needed.

2. Cut four 6-inch rounds of parchment paper. Roll out the dough on a lightly

This recipe appeared in the January/February 2002 issue of Shooting Sportsman magazine. Herbes de Provence is a mixture of herbs from the Provence region of France, and consists of a blend of lavender, tarragon, rosemary, thyme, basil, savory, fennel and marjoram. I find that it works especially well with duck and chicken. If you have access to specialty mushrooms you can substitute for the portabellas; note that delicate mushrooms like oysters or trumpets will cook much faster. I purchase my herbes de Provence from Penzey's (see Mail Order Sources, page 242). ∎

floured surface to $^1/_8$-inch thick. Cut into four $5^1/_2$-inch circles and form into 4-inch tartlet pans (with removable bottoms) that have been sprayed (or brushed) with vegetable oil. The dough should evenly coat the bottom and sides of the tartlet mold. Reserve the remaining dough for another use.

3. Place the 6-inch parchment round on top of each tartlet and fill with dry beans or pie weights. Bake in a preheated 350-degree oven for 15 minutes. Remove the tartlets from the oven and empty out the beans or pie weights and parchment paper. Return the tartlets to the oven for 10 more minutes to lightly brown.

4. In a large skillet, heat the olive oil over medium heat. Clean the mushrooms and cut into $^1/_2$-inch dice. Add the chopped onion to the skillet and cook for 1 minute, stirring occasionally. Add mushrooms and garlic and cook for 3 minutes, stirring occasionally.

5. Remove from the heat and pour the mixture into a fine mesh strainer, reserving the juices in a bowl beneath. Toss occasionally to allow all of the excess moisture to drain through.

6. For the sauce, return the pan to the stove and deglaze with the sherry. Reduce until dry. Add the cream and reserved mushroom juices and reduce by half. Remove from the heat and whisk in the soft butter. Taste, and season with salt and white pepper if necessary. Strain sauce through a fine strainer and reserve in a warm place.

7. Preheat the oven to 350 degrees. In a hot cast-iron skillet, sear the duck breast, skin side down first for about 5 minutes. Turn the breast over and brown the other side for 5 minutes. Transfer to a small ovenproof pan/plate and finish cooking in the preheated oven until it is medium-rare (pink inside) about 5–7 minutes.

8. Place the prepared tartlet shells on a small baking sheet. Season the "dry"

mushroom mixture with salt and white pepper and divide between the shells. Sprinkle the top of each tartlet with 1 teaspoon of grated Parmesan cheese and bake in a 350-degree oven for 10 minutes.

9. To serve, remove the tartlet from its tin and place it in the center of a 10-inch plate. Slice the duck breast and fan half of the breast on each tartlet. Drizzle the sauce over and around the tartlet. Garnish the plate with tomato strips and chopped chives.

This dish earned me the title of "Caribbean Chef of the Year" and was featured in USA Today on November 8, 1996. I created this dish for the competition because of its Caribbean feeling, colorful use of island fruits, the contrasting textures of the crisp plantain and the shrimp, and the sweet, sour and spicy flavors in the marinade, sauce and salsa. It proved to be a winning combination. ■

PLANTAIN SHRIMP WITH A PASSION FRUIT SAUCE

SERVES 4

MARINADE

12 EXTRA-LARGE RAW SHRIMP, PEELED AND DEVEINED
1/4 HABANERO CHILI, MINCED
2 CLOVES GARLIC, MINCED
1 TEASPOON CHOPPED CILANTRO
2 TABLESPOONS CANOLA OIL
1 LIME, JUICED
1 TABLESPOON SWEET CHILI SAUCE
1/2 OUNCE WHITE WINE VINEGAR
1/2 TEASPOON KOSHER SALT
1/4 TEASPOON GROUND BLACK PEPPER

PASSION FRUIT SAUCE

1/2 TEASPOON GROUND ANNATTO SEEDS
    (ALSO KNOWN AS ACHIOTE)
1 TABLESPOON CANOLA OIL

1 TEASPOON GRANULATED SUGAR

2 PASSION FRUITS, SEEDS AND JUICE (RESERVE HALF OF ONE
FOR GARNISH) OR USE $1/4$ CUP PASSION FRUIT CONCENTRATE

1 OUNCE WHITE WINE VINEGAR

$1/2$ LIME, JUICED

2 CUPS WATER (RESERVE 2 TABLESPOONS WATER)

$1/2$ TEASPOON CORNSTARCH

SALT AND WHITE PEPPER TO TASTE

COATING AND GARNISH

FLOUR FOR DUSTING SHRIMP

2 GREEN PLANTAINS, PEELED

4 SPRIGS CILANTRO FOR GARNISH

1 BATCH MANGO-CILANTRO SALSA (RECIPE, PAGE 89)

1. Mix together all the marinade ingredients and toss in the shrimp. Marinate for at least 30 minutes.

2. For the passion fruit sauce, heat the oil in a small saucepan. Add the ground annatto and cook briefly to extract the color. Add the sugar, passion fruit seeds and juice, vinegar, lime juice and water. Bring mixture to a boil. Mix the reserved 2 Tablespoons of water with the cornstarch into what is known as a slurry. Whisk the slurry into the boiling sauce to thicken it. Cook for 5 minutes on low heat. Season with salt and white pepper. Reserve.

3. Slice the plantains lengthwise, thinly, using a mandoline. Drain the marinade off the shrimp. Dust with flour and wrap each shrimp with a plantain strip. Hold together with a toothpick or skewer. Deep-fry in 350-degree oil until plantain is crisp and shrimp is cooked, about 2 minutes. Serve the shrimp over the Passion fruit sauce with mounds of Mango-cilantro salsa and garnish with cilantro sprigs.

Passion fruit is a fruit like no other. This small, round tropical fruit has a thin purple outside shell, and when cut in half, exposes a hollow inside with tiny black seeds that are surrounded by a soft yellow membrane. To extract the juice from the fruit, cut it in half and scoop the seeds and juice into a strainer set over a bowl. Gently press on the seeds to release the juices. If you can't find the fresh fruit in your area, Welch's makes a passion fruit concentrate that is widely available. ■

Maine Crab and Shrimp Cakes with a Caribbean Remoulade

Peeky Toe crabmeat is the most flavorful crabmeat available in our area. It makes terrific crab cakes. I also add cooked Maine shrimp to the crab cakes, which provides more texture to the mix. The panko breadcrumbs are worth searching for since they coat the cakes with so much more crunch than regular breadcrumbs would. Panko breadcrumbs are available at Asian markets and well-stocked supermarkets. ■

SERVES 6

1/2 POUND MAINE SHRIMP MEAT (TITI OR SMALL RAW SHRIMP)
2 TABLESPOONS OLIVE OIL
3/4 POUND FRESH MAINE CRABMEAT (PREFERABLY
    PEEKY TOE CRABMEAT)
1 LARGE EGG
1 TABLESPOON MINCED RED ONION
2 TABLESPOONS FINELY CHOPPED CELERY
2 TABLESPOONS FINELY CHOPPED RED BELL PEPPER
1/2 CUP MAYONNAISE
1 1/2 CUPS PANKO BREAD CRUMBS (JAPANESE)
1/2 TEASPOON FRESH THYME LEAVES, CHOPPED
1/2 TEASPOON CARIBBEAN DRY SPICE MIX (RECIPE, PAGE 169)
12 EXTRA-LARGE RAW SHRIMP, PEELED AND DEVEINED
1 TEASPOON OLIVE OIL
2 CLOVES GARLIC, MINCED
KOSHER SALT AND FRESHLY GROUND BLACK PEPPER
2 TABLESPOONS CANOLA OIL
CARIBBEAN REMOULADE (RECIPE FOLLOWS)
SWEET CORN RELISH (RECIPE FOLLOWS)
6 FRESH THYME SPRIGS FOR GARNISH

1. Drain the Maine shrimp and remove any shell fragments. Pat dry with paper towels.

2. In a medium sauté pan, heat the olive oil over medium-high heat and sauté the Maine shrimp for 1 minute. Squeeze the excess water from the crabmeat, and

place the crabmeat in a large bowl. Add the cooked shrimp, egg, red onion, celery, red bell pepper, mayonnaise, $1/2$ cup of the panko breadcrumbs, thyme and Caribbean dry spice mix. Stir to combine.

3. Portion the crabmeat mixture into 12 balls and pat down, forming the balls into $3/4$-inch high disks. One by one, set the cakes into a bowl with the remaining panko breadcrumbs to coat, pressing lightly and coating on both sides.

4. Preheat the oven to 300 degrees. Coat the shrimp with the olive oil, garlic and salt and pepper.

5. Heat a large skillet over medium-high heat. Sauté the crab cakes in 2 Tablespoons canola oil for 2 minutes on each side, until golden brown. Transfer to a baking sheet and keep warm in a 300-degree oven.

6. Wipe out the sauté pan with a paper towel and return to the heat. When hot, add the shrimp and cook for 30 seconds on each side, or until they become opaque.

7. To serve, place two crab cakes in the center of the plates, leaning one of them on the other. Place a 2-Tablespoon dollop of Caribbean remoulade in front of the crab cakes and a mound of Sweet corn relish behind them. Place a shrimp on the top of each crab cake. Garnish with fresh thyme sprigs.

CARIBBEAN REMOULADE

1/2 CUP MAYONNAISE
1/2 TEASPOON CARIBBEAN DRY SPICE MIX
1 TABLESPOON FINELY CHOPPED RED BELL PEPPER
1 TEASPOON CAPERS, CHOPPED
PINCH OF SALT

1. Combine all ingredients and mix well. *Can be made up to 2 days in advance if covered and refrigerated.*

SWEET CORN RELISH

2 EARS FRESH CORN ON THE COB
1 TABLESPOON MINCED RED ONION
2 TABLESPOONS FINELY CHOPPED RED BELL PEPPER
3 TABLESPOONS COARSELY CHOPPED CILANTRO
1 LIME, JUICED
2 TEASPOONS EXTRA VIRGIN OLIVE OIL
KOSHER SALT AND FRESHLY GROUND BLACK PEPPER TO TASTE

1. Cut the corn off the cob and blanch in a small pot of salted boiling water for 2 minutes. Strain off water and place the corn in a medium-sized bowl. Spread out to cool. Add the remaining ingredients and toss. The relish should be made at least 2 hours in advance to allow the flavors to combine. *It can be made up to 2 days in advance if covered and refrigerated.*

ℋ

I accompany my Crab and shrimp cakes with both a remoulade and a vegetable relish. The Caribbean remoulade is very simple to make and uses my Caribbean dry spice mix (page 169). The Sweet corn relish is perfect for summer months when fresh corn on the cob is readily available. In the spring, I serve the crab cakes with an asparagus relish while in the fall a fresh beet or parsnip relish may complement the cakes. ■

Soups

BUTTERNUT SQUASH SOUP WITH A NUTMEG CREAM

SERVES 8

2 1/2 POUNDS BUTTERNUT SQUASH, SKIN AND SEEDS REMOVED,
    ROUGHLY CUT INTO 1/2-INCH CUBES
2 MEDIUM CARROTS, PEELED AND ROUGHLY CUT INTO
    1/2-INCH CUBES
2 TABLESPOONS CANOLA OIL
2 MEDIUM-SIZED YELLOW ONIONS, PEELED AND ROUGHLY CUT
1 STALK CELERY, ROUGHLY CUT
1 1/2 QUARTS CHICKEN STOCK
1 BAY LEAF
1/4 TEASPOON THYME LEAVES
1 1/2 TEASPOONS BROWN SUGAR, FIRMLY PACKED
SALT AND WHITE PEPPER TO TASTE
1/4 CUP WHIPPING CREAM
1 DASH FRESHLY GRATED NUTMEG
KOSHER SALT AND WHITE PEPPER TO TASTE
2 TEASPOONS CHOPPED CHIVES
1/4 CUP CRISP CROUTONS

1. Preheat the oven to 400 degrees.

2. Place the cut butternut squash and carrots on an oiled baking sheet and roast
   in the preheated oven for 1 hour.

3. Heat the oil in a large (4-quart) saucepan. Add the onions and cook for
   3 minutes, stirring occasionally. Stir in roasted squash and carrots, celery,
   chicken stock, bay leaf, thyme and brown sugar. Bring to a boil, and reduce
   to a simmer for about 30 minutes.

The best way to remove the skin from a butternut squash is to first remove both ends of the squash with a large knife. Lay the squash down on the cutting board and cut the squash in half, dividing the top skinny part from the rounded base with the seeds. Now you can use either a vegetable peeler, going over the squash several times to remove all of the skin, or a large knife, following the contour of the squash as it sits upright on the cutting board. ■

Bisques are thick, rich soups usually made from shellfish like shrimp, crab and lobster. If you live in an area where crab and shrimp are more abundant or you simply prefer to make a shrimp bisque or a crab bisque, make the following changes. Cook four crabs as in step 1 for 6 minutes (shells will turn bright red when done), pick crabmeat from body and claws and reserve, rinse shells and begin with step 2, omitting the picking of the meat. For shrimp bisque, remove the shells from 2 pounds of medium shrimp and reserve. Poach the shrimp in the fish stock for 3 minutes, devein and reserve for step 5. Continue with step 2, using shrimp shells instead of lobster, omitting the picking of the meat. ∎

4. Remove from the heat and discard the bay leaf. Blend the soup with either a handheld immersion blender or in a regular household blender until smooth. Season with salt and white pepper.

5. To serve, whip the cream to stiff peaks and season with nutmeg, salt and white pepper. Ladle soup into serving bowls and top with a dollop of whipped cream. Sprinkle with chopped chives and crisp croutons.

LOBSTER BISQUE

SERVES 4

TWO 1¼ POUND LIVE MAINE LOBSTERS
4 TABLESPOONS UNSALTED BUTTER
1 MEDIUM YELLOW ONION
1 CUP SMALL DICE CARROTS
1 STALK CELERY, SMALL DICE
½ CUP ALL-PURPOSE FLOUR
2 TABLESPOONS TOMATO PASTE
¼ CUP COGNAC
1 CUP DRY WHITE WINE
1 BAY LEAF
¼ TEASPOON FRESH THYME LEAVES
5 CUPS LOBSTER OR FISH STOCK
½ CUP HEAVY CREAM
SALT AND WHITE PEPPER TO TASTE
½ CUP HEAVY CREAM, FOR WHIPPING
KOSHER SALT AND WHITE PEPPER TO TASTE
1 TEASPOON COGNAC
½ TEASPOON FRESH THYME LEAVES FOR GARNISH

1. First prepare the lobster. Bring 1 gallon of water to a boil in a large (9-quart) stockpot. Submerge the lobsters, head first, into the water and cook for 2 minutes, covered. Remove and cool. Split the lobster in half lengthwise by placing it on its back and cutting with a large chef's knife from its head down through the body and tail. Remove the claws and arm sections and separate. Remove the tail section from the body and remove the vein (discard). Rinse the body halves under a faucet briefly, removing the green liver (tamale). Cut the lobster body halves into 3 pieces each. Place all of the lobster pieces in a strainer to drain and dry. Reserve.

2. In a 4-quart saucepan over medium-high heat, melt 4 Tablespoons of butter and sauté the chopped onion, carrots and celery. Cook for 2 minutes, stirring occasionally. Add the dried lobster pieces and cook for another 7 minutes, stirring occasionally. Lobster pieces should turn red and the meat should cook through. Remove the lobster pieces with meat in them (tail, claw and arm pieces) and let cool until you can remove the meat from the shells. Return the shells to the pan, reserving the lobster meat.

3. Turn the heat down to a medium flame and add the flour to the pan. Stir to coat the lobster pieces and vegetables. Cook for 2 minutes stirring constantly. Add the tomato paste and cook for 2 more minutes, stirring constantly. Add the cognac and flame. Extinguish with the white wine and cook briefly. Add the bay leaf, thyme, and lobster or fish stock. Bring the soup to a boil over medium heat and reduce down to a simmer. Simmer for 20 minutes.

4. Strain the soup through a fine mesh strainer, pressing on the lobster and vegetables to release as many juices as possible. Return to a clean saucepan and add $1/2$ cup of the heavy cream. Season with salt and white pepper.

5. To serve, whip the other $1/2$ cup of heavy cream to stiff peaks and season with salt, white pepper and 1 teaspoon cognac. Cut the reserved lobster meat into

$^1/_2$-inch pieces and divide between the bowls. Ladle the soup into the bowls and garnish with a spoonful of whipped cream and a sprinkling of fresh thyme leaves.

Chilled Summer Gazpacho with an Herbed Sour Cream

SERVES 8

2 MEDIUM-SIZED BEEFSTEAK TOMATOES
1 SMALL VIDALIA ONION
$^1/_2$ ENGLISH CUCUMBER (ALSO KNOWN AS SEEDLESS CUCUMBERS)
$^1/_2$ RED BELL PEPPER
2 SCALLIONS
32 OUNCES TOMATO JUICE
8 OUNCES V8 JUICE
2 TABLESPOONS EXTRA VIRGIN OLIVE OIL
$^1/_4$ CUP RICE WINE VINEGAR
$^1/_8$ TEASPOON FRESHLY GROUND BLACK PEPPER
SALT TO TASTE

1. Core the tomatoes, cut them in half across the equator to expose the seeds and gently squeeze out the seeds. Dice the tomatoes, onion, cucumber and bell pepper into $^1/_2$-inch cubes. Finely slice the scallions. Combine all the ingredients, mix and refrigerate, covered, for at least 2 hours. *May be made up to 2 days in advance.*

Gazpacho is a refreshing soup for a hot summer day. I usually make gazpacho one day in advance to allow the flavors in the soup to blend. The herbed sour cream enhances the soup with additional body and the Caribbean dry spice mix gives the soup a little zing. Maine summers are quite short, limiting the tomato growing season, so I focus on small varieties like sungold, red and yellow pears and small, red cherry tomatoes. These small tomatoes are perfect for garnishing the soup. ■

HERBED SOUR CREAM

1/2 CUP SOUR CREAM
2 TEASPOONS CHOPPED FRESH CILANTRO
1 SCALLION, GREEN PART ONLY, FINELY CHOPPED
1/2 TEASPOON CARIBBEAN DRY SPICE MIX (RECIPE, PAGE 169)
SALT TO TASTE

1. Mix all together.

PRESENTATION

8 RED CHERRY TOMATOES, CUT IN HALF
2 MEDIUM-SIZED GOLDEN TOMATOES, CUT INTO 8 WEDGES
8 SPRIGS CILANTRO

1. Ladle the soup into the desired serving bowls and decorate with a dollop of the herbed sour cream, 2 cherry tomato halves and 2 golden tomato wedges. Top with a sprig of cilantro and serve.

POTATO AND LEEK SOUP WITH WHITE TRUFFLE OIL

SERVES 6

1/2 POUND LEEKS, WHITE AND LIGHT GREEN PARTS ONLY,
   SLICED (ABOUT 3 CUPS)
2 TABLESPOONS UNSALTED BUTTER
1/2 CUP CHOPPED YELLOW ONIONS
2 GARLIC CLOVES, MINCED
1 POUND RED POTATOES, PEELED AND CUT INTO 1-INCH DICE
   (ABOUT 2 1/2 CUPS)

Potato and leek soup is a nice hearty soup for a cold fall or winter day. The croutons I use at the Inn are made from excess sour dough bread that remains at the end of the evening. Using a serrated knife, I start by cutting the bread into 1/2-inch cubes. For every cup of cubed bread, heat 2 Tablespoons of extra virgin olive oil in a large sauté pan set over medium heat. When the oil is hot, add the cubed bread and cook over medium heat, stirring frequently until the cubes are golden brown. Season with kosher salt. ■

4 CUPS CHICKEN STOCK
1 BAY LEAF
1 SPRIG FRESH THYME
SALT AND WHITE PEPPER TO TASTE
4 TEASPOONS WHITE TRUFFLE OIL
1 TABLESPOON COARSELY CHOPPED ITALIAN PARSLEY LEAVES
1/4 CUP CRISP CROUTONS

1. Thoroughly soak, wash and drain the water from the leeks.

2. In a 4-quart saucepan, melt the butter and sauté the onions for 5 minutes over medium heat. Add the garlic and cook for 2 minutes and then add the leeks and cook for 4 more minutes.

3. Add the potatoes, chicken stock, bay leaf and fresh thyme sprig. Bring to a boil and simmer for 30 minutes.

4. Remove the bay leaf and thyme sprig. Puree the soup with either an immersion blender or a regular household blender until smooth. Adjust seasoning with salt and white pepper.

5. Ladle the soup into the desired serving bowls. Drizzle with the white truffle oil and sprinkle with the Italian parsley and croutons.

Corn and Lobster Chowder with Crisp Bacon

SERVES 6

TWO 1½ POUND LIVE MAINE LOBSTERS
6 STRIPS THICK-SLICED BACON (SPECIALTY SMOKED IF AVAILABLE)
2 TABLESPOONS OLIVE OIL
1 CUP FINELY CHOPPED YELLOW ONION

Chowders, of course, are quintessential New England. Maine is especially known for its clam, fish and seafood chowders. Lobster and corn combine to create an exceptional chowder that is creamy, rich and hearty, with tender chunks of potatoes and finished off with crisp-smoky bacon. It's hard to beat. ■

2 TABLESPOONS UNSALTED BUTTER

1/4 CUP ALL-PURPOSE FLOUR

1/2 TEASPOON FRESHLY GROUND BLACK PEPPER

1 BAY LEAF

2 CUPS MEDIUM DICE RED SKIN POTATOES,
    WASHED AND NOT PEELED

1/2 CUP SMALL DICE CARROTS

4 EARS CORN ON THE COB

1 CUP HEAVY CREAM

SALT TO TASTE

1 TABLESPOON PICKED ITALIAN PARSLEY LEAVES

1. Fill a large 9-quart stockpot with two inches of water, cover and bring to a boil. Add live lobsters, cover and cook for 10 minutes. Remove from the water and let cool. When cool, crack lobsters and remove the meat from the claws, knuckles and tail (discarding the vein). Cut the lobster meat into 1/2-inch pieces. Reserve lobster meat and shells separately, washing the green tamale away.

2. Pour the cooking liquid from the pot into a quart measurer. Fill to 1 quart, using additional water if necessary. Place the lobster heads and shells in the large pot with the 1 quart of cooking liquid. Bring to a boil and simmer for 15 minutes. Strain and reserve the liquid, discarding the shells.

3. Cut the bacon into 1/2-inch pieces. Heat the olive oil in a 4-quart saucepan over medium-high heat. Add the bacon, stirring occasionally, and cook until crisp. Scoop out the crisp bacon (reserve) and add the onions and butter. Cook the onions until translucent. Stir in the flour and cook for 3 minutes, stirring frequently. Whisk in the reserved lobster stock and add the bay leaf, black pepper and diced potatoes. Cook for 15 minutes and add the diced carrots. Cook for 5 more minutes.

4. Remove the husk and hair from the ears of corn. Cut each ear in half width-wise. Stand the halves on the cut ends and remove the kernels of corn with a chef's knife, following close to the cob. Add the corn to the soup and cook for an additional 5 minutes.

5. Remove the bay leaf from the soup and stir in the heavy cream. Adjust seasoning with the salt.

6. Add the lobster meat to the soup, set over low heat, 2 minutes before serving. Ladle the soup into the serving bowls. Garnish with picked Italian parsley leaves and serve.

White Bean Soup with Pancetta

SERVES 8–10

1 POUND NAVY BEANS
3 TABLESPOONS OLIVE OIL
1 POUND PANCETTA
3 TABLESPOONS UNSALTED BUTTER
1 HAM HOCK
2 CUPS CHOPPED YELLOW ONIONS
4 CLOVES GARLIC, MINCED
7 CUPS CHICKEN STOCK
1 BAY LEAF
1 LARGE SPRIG FRESH THYME
1½ MEDIUM-SIZED CARROTS, SMALL DICE (1 CUP)
2 STALKS CELERY, SMALL DICE (1 CUP)
SALT AND WHITE PEPPER
2 TEASPOONS FRESH THYME LEAVES FOR GARNISH

Pancetta is Italian bacon (made from pork fat back) that is cured with salt and spices, but is not smoked. The cured pork fat back is tightly rolled creating a large "Genoa salami" sized roll. Unlike other Italian charcuterie products like prosciutto, capicola, and salami, pancetta is raw and needs to be cooked. Specialty food stores or Italian markets usually carry pancetta in their deli sections. Ask them to slice it for you into ¼-inch thick slices. ■

1. Soak the navy beans overnight in 2 quarts of water.

2. Heat the 3 Tablespoons of olive oil in a 9-quart stockpot over medium heat. Dice the pancetta into $1/4$-inch cubes, and cook it gently in the olive oil (stirring often) until it turns golden brown and crisp. With a slotted spoon, remove the pancetta from the pan and reserve, leaving the fat in the saucepan.

3. Add the butter to the saucepan used for the pancetta. When it has melted, add the ham hock and cook for 5 minutes, turning it to brown on all sides. Add the chopped onion and cook for 3 minutes. Add the garlic and stir, cooking for 30 seconds.

4. Drain the water from the soaking beans and add the beans, chicken stock, bay leaf and fresh thyme to the onion mixture. Cook the soup over medium heat for 1 hour.

5. Remove the ham hock from the soup and cut away the meat, discarding the tendons, skin and bone. Finely dice the meat from the ham hock and add it to the soup. Remove and discard the bay leaf and thyme sprig.

6. Puree the soup with either an immersion blender or a regular household blender until it has become thick, and is still rather chunky. Add the diced carrots and continue to cook the soup for 10 minutes, stirring occasionally. Add the celery and cook for 5 minutes. Adjust seasoning with salt and white pepper.

7. Ladle the soup into the desired serving bowls. Sprinkle with the crisp pancetta and fresh thyme.

Salads

CRABMEAT TIMBALE WITH BABY GREENS AND A PAPAYA SEED DRESSING

SERVES 4

1 POUND FRESH CRABMEAT
1 TABLESPOON WHOLE GRAIN MUSTARD
1/2 CUP WHIPPING CREAM, WHIPPED
1/2 TEASPOON MINCED LEMON ZEST
1 TABLESPOON LEMON JUICE
SALT AND WHITE PEPPER TO TASTE
1/4 CUP CANOLA OIL
1/2 CUP RICE FLOUR STICKS (VERMICELLI) BROKEN INTO
   2-INCH PIECES
5 OUNCES BABY GREENS (MESCLUN MIX), WASHED AND DRIED
PAPAYA SEED DRESSING (RECIPE, PAGE 126)
CUCUMBER SLICES, RED RADISH WEDGES AND PAPAYA SLICES
   FOR GARNISH

1. Squeeze the excess water from the crabmeat and place in a medium-sized mixing bowl. Pick through to remove any shell fragments that remain. Add the mustard, whipped cream, lemon zest and juice, and mix gently to combine. Season with salt and white pepper. Reserve.

2. In a small skillet, heat the canola oil until it is smoking hot. Have a slotted spoon and a plate with a few sheets of paper towel on it next to the stove. Add half of the rice sticks to the hot oil; they will puff; as they do, remove them

Rice flour sticks, also known as rice flour noodles, are widely available at Asian markets and some supermarkets. Rice sticks come in various sizes, from very fine (like angel hair) to 1/2-inch wide noodles, and are used in Chinese soups and stir fries. ∎

immediately from the oil with the slotted spoon and drain on the paper towels. Repeat with the remaining rice sticks. Sprinkle with a little kosher salt.

3. To serve, line four small ramekins with plastic wrap (to keep the crabmeat from sticking) and divide the crabmeat mixture between them, compacting it to make a firm mold. Invert the timbale onto the center of a chilled salad plate, removing the ramekin and plastic wrap. Toss the greens with enough dressing to lightly coat each leaf and arrange around the timbale. Garnish with the cucumber slices, radish wedges, papaya slices and crisp rice sticks.

AVOCADO AND PAPAYA SALAD

SERVES 4–6

1/4 CUP WHITE WINE VINEGAR
2 TABLESPOONS FRESH LIME JUICE
1 TEASPOON DIJON-STYLE MUSTARD
1/4 CUP EXTRA VIRGIN OLIVE OIL
4 AVOCADOS, RIPE
4 HAWAIIAN PAPAYAS, RIPE (OR 1 LARGE CARIBBEAN PAPAYA, ABOUT 3 1/2 POUNDS)
2 TABLESPOONS COARSELY CHOPPED CILANTRO
SALT AND FRESHLY GROUND BLACK PEPPER TO TASTE
2 LIMES CUT INTO WEDGES AND 6 CILANTRO SPRIGS FOR GARNISH

Hawaiian papayas are more readily available than the large papayas found throughout the Caribbean. As long as they're ripe, either type will work well in this colorful and delicious Caribbean-inspired salad. Top the salad with grilled shrimp to create a refreshing summer lunch entrée. ▪

1. Whisk together the vinegar, lime juice and mustard. While whisking vigorously, drizzle in the olive oil.

2. Cut the avocados and papayas in half. Remove and discard the avocado pit and remove the papaya seeds. Scoop out the flesh of the avocado and papaya using a melon baller.

Baby Greens from Hummalong Farm

INDEPENDENCE, the pleasure of physical labor, the ability to work the land—not to mention winters off—keep Clive Poole and Mary Schulien content running Hummalong Farm on seven acres of fields and woods in North Appleton, Maine. Clive and Mary, who have been married 30 years, built their home, a barn and a workshop on the site, which was part of a larger farm until the 1940s. The couple developed the garden plots and began farming there in 1990, concentrating on salad and specialty greens they sell to several mid-coast Maine restaurants and caterers. In addition to the tender, succulent greens, Clive and Mary grow summer and winter squash, onions and leeks—for sale at their stand at the Camden Farmer's Market.

Farming suits them, they say, because it advantageously combines their talents. Clive prepares the garden and does the planting, weeding and harvesting while Mary handles the packaging and sales, and pitches in with weeding and harvesting. In the off-season, they kick back, run a winter caretaking business and wait for the snow. Says Mary, "To everything there is a season."

3. Mix papaya and avocado balls together in a bowl and gently toss in the dressing with the chopped cilantro. Season to taste with salt and black pepper. Garnish with lime wedges and cilantro sprigs.

GINGER CHICKEN SALAD

SERVES 4

3 BONELESS AND SKINLESS CHICKEN BREASTS
1 BATCH GINGER DRESSING (RECIPE FOLLOWS)
8 WONTON WRAPPERS
2 CUPS CANOLA OIL, FOR FRYING
KOSHER SALT TO TASTE
1 HEAD OF ROMAINE HEARTS
3 CUPS SHREDDED NAPA (CHINESE) CABBAGE
1½ CUPS SNOW PEAS
1 MEDIUM CARROT
3 SCALLIONS, GREEN PART ONLY
½ RED BELL PEPPER
1 TABLESPOON SESAME SEEDS, TOASTED
2 TEASPOONS BLACK SESAME SEEDS

This recipe produces four large "lunch-sized" portions of salad. If you intend for this salad to be one of many courses in a meal, safely assume that this recipe will feed from 8–10 people. Everything can be made well in advance and tossed together at the last minute. To toast the sesame seeds for the salad, heat a small sauté pan over medium-low heat and add the sesame seeds. Toss frequently, toasting the seeds until they are lightly browned.

1. Trim any fat from the chicken breasts and marinate in ¼-cup of the Ginger dressing for 1 hour.

2. Cut the wonton wrappers into quarters, cutting from corner to corner, creating small triangles.

3. Heat the oil over medium-high heat, to 350 degrees, or until a drop of water reacts violently when dropped into the oil. Separate the triangles of wonton wrappers, and gently place them into the hot oil. Fry in small batches until

golden brown and crisp. Remove to a plate lined with paper towel and sprinkle with kosher salt. Reserve.

4. Cut the core from the romaine hearts and separate the leaves. Wash well and either spin in a salad spinner or pat dry with a clean kitchen towel. Tear the romaine leaves into 1-inch pieces and place in a large bowl with the shredded Napa cabbage.

5. In a 4-quart saucepan, boil 2 quarts of water. Snap the ends and strings from the snow peas. Cut each pea in half width-wise on a bias. Prepare a mixing bowl with 2 cups of cold water and 1 cup of ice to shock the peas. When the water is boiling, drop in the peas and cook for 15 seconds. Remove immediately to the bowl of ice water to stop the cooking and set in the bright green color. Cool completely. Remove from the water and pat dry.

6. Peel and julienne the carrot using a julienne peeler, a mandoline or a chef's knife. A julienne cut is a long thin strip, $1/8$ inch by $1/8$ inch by 2 inches long. Wash the scallions and slice them on the bias into $1/4$-inch slices. Remove the seeds from the bell pepper and cut off the top and bottom of the pepper, leaving a uniform strip from the center of the pepper. Slice down the pepper so it will lay down flat on the work surface and remove any of the white ribbing with a sharp paring knife. Slice the pepper into thin strips.

7. Heat a grill pan over medium-high heat. Grill the chicken breasts for about 6–7 minutes on each side, or until cooked through. Do not overcook, or chicken will be tough. Remove the chicken to a cutting board and let the juices settle for 2 minutes before slicing. Slice into $1/4$-inch thin strips.

8. To serve, toss the romaine and Napa with black and white sesame seeds and enough of the remaining Ginger dressing to coat it well. Divide among four plates. Decoratively arrange the chicken breast, red bell pepper, carrots, snow peas and scallions on the salads. Drizzle the chicken and snow peas

with some of the extra dressing and top with the crisp wonton wrappers.
Serve immediately.

GINGER DRESSING

MAKES 1 ½ CUPS

½ CUP RICE WINE VINEGAR
¼ CUP SOY SAUCE
1½ TABLESPOONS HOISIN SAUCE
1 TEASPOON DRY MUSTARD POWDER
1 TEASPOON GRANULATED SUGAR
1 TABLESPOON MINCED GINGER
1 TABLESPOON MINCED SHALLOTS
½ TEASPOON MINCED GARLIC
2 TABLESPOONS SESAME OIL
⅓ CUP CANOLA OIL

1. Combine all the ingredients, except for the oils, in a blender. Blend for
30 seconds to combine well. With the blender still running, drizzle in the
two oils and blend for an additional 10 seconds.

SALAD DRESSINGS

½ CUP WHITE WINE VINEGAR
½ CUP GRANULATED SUGAR
½ CUP CANOLA OIL
¼ CUP CHOPPED VIDALIA ONION
½ TEASPOON KOSHER SALT
½ TEASPOON DRY MUSTARD

This is a good basic foundation recipe for fruit-based dressings. My friend Carol gave me the inspiration for this recipe and introduced me to using papaya seeds in dressings. Experiment with other fruit combinations if you don't see your favorite fruit here. These dressings will keep for several weeks in the refrigerator. ■

1. Select the flavor of dressing you wish to prepare from the list below.

2. Combine all the ingredients above, making the required changes as noted below, in a blender and mix until smooth.

RASPBERRY-CHIVE: Substitute raspberry vinegar for the white wine vinegar and add $1/2$ cup fresh or frozen raspberries and 1 Tablespoon chopped fresh chives

NECTARINE-BLACK PEPPER: Add one ripe nectarine, pitted and coarsely chopped, and 1 teaspoon freshly ground black pepper

BLUEBERRY-GINGER: Add $1/2$ cup fresh or frozen blueberries and 1 teaspoon freshly minced ginger

KIWI: Add 2 peeled and coarsely chopped ripe kiwis and 2 teaspoons chopped flat leaf parsley

PAPAYA SEED: Substitute rice wine vinegar for the white wine vinegar and add $1/2$ cup chopped fresh papaya and 1 Tablespoon papaya seeds

APPLE-MAPLE: Substitute cider vinegar for the white wine vinegar and add $1^1/2$ Tablespoons real maple syrup and 2 small apples (Cortland and Galas work well), cored and coarsely chopped

MANGO-LIME: Add the flesh from $1/2$ mango, removing the skin and seeds, and the juice and finely grated zest from one lime

Borealis Breads

IF THERE IS a first name in Maine baking, it's got to be Borealis Bread, the company founder Jim Amaral happily calls "the Van Gogh of dough." As a kid, Amaral worked as the doughnut dipper at a bakery in Concord, Massachusetts. Later in life, he detoured through restaurant kitchens, a wine-making stint and a few years baking sourdough breads in Seattle, Washington. But when Amaral hit Maine in 1993, the bread idea began to rise, and he started a small company called Bodacious Breads in downtown Waldoboro.

Ten years later, Bodacious has become Borealis, and Amaral runs a somewhat bigger company, with four retail locations throughout the state—one in Waldoboro, one in the southern Maine town of Wells and two in Portland. Borealis products are instantly recognizable by their crusty exteriors and deliciously moist and chewy interiors. The breads, including olive, rosemary, Aroostook wheat, sourdough baguette and Italian, are increasingly made from organic wheat grown by Maine farmers, part of Amaral's commitment to sustainable agriculture and delicious food.

We serve a fruit sorbet every evening at the Inn as a cleansing course before the entrée. Any fruit can be used for sorbet, you just need to consider the type of flesh or juice a fruit produces, and match it to one of these recipes. I use a simple electric ice cream machine that spins an insulated freezer bowl. You plug it in, pull the frozen freezer bowl out of your freezer and place it on the machine, place the lid on top, turn it on and pour in the ingredients. In about 20 minutes you have sorbet. Transfer the sorbet to a plastic container with a lid and let it freeze for at least 2 hours to set up firm. ■

ARTSTONE SORBET

SIMPLE SYRUP

    4 CUPS WATER
    4 CUPS GRANULATED SUGAR

1. Bring the water and sugar to a boil in a 4-quart saucepan, giving it a gentle stir every 30 seconds. Once the boil is reached, reduce the heat to low and simmer for 5 minutes. Remove from the heat and cool. Use the simple syrup in the recipes below to prepare many different flavors of sorbet.

LEMON SORBET

    1 CUP LEMON JUICE
    1 TABLESPOON MINCED LEMON ZEST
    2 CUPS SIMPLE SYRUP (RECIPE ABOVE)

1. Combine all the ingredients in a bowl and refrigerate for 2 hours to cool. Prepare your ice cream maker for freezing, and follow the manufacturer's instructions for making sorbet/ice cream.

BERRY SORBET

> 1/4 CUP LEMON JUICE
> 1 POUND FRESH OR FROZEN BERRIES (FOR STRAWBERRIES, REMOVE STEMS AND CUT INTO 1/2-INCH PIECES)
> 1/4 CUP LIGHT CORN SYRUP
> 2 CUPS SIMPLE SYRUP (RECIPE, OPPOSITE PAGE)

1. Place the lemon juice and berries in a food processor or blender, and puree until very smooth, about 2 minutes. Strain the berry mixture through a fine mesh strainer to remove the seeds. Combine the strained berry juice with the remaining ingredients in a bowl and refrigerate for 2 hours to cool. Prepare your ice cream maker for freezing, and follow the manufacturer's instructions for making sorbet/ice cream.

PEACH, MANGO OR PAPAYA SORBET

> 1/4 CUP LEMON JUICE
> 1 POUND FRESH OR FROZEN PEACHES, MANGOES OR PAPAYAS (REMOVE SKINS, SEEDS AND PITS)
> 1/4 CUP LIGHT CORN SYRUP
> 2 CUPS SIMPLE SYRUP (RECIPE, OPPOSITE PAGE)

1. Place the lemon juice and fruit in a food processor or blender, and puree until very smooth, about 2 minutes. Combine the fruit puree and the remaining ingredients in a bowl and refrigerate for 2 hours to cool. Prepare your ice cream maker for freezing, and follow the manufacturer's instructions for making sorbet/ice cream.

Entrées

MAINE LOBSTER WITH A VANILLA BEURRE BLANC

SERVES 4

FOUR 1½ POUND LIVE MAINE LOBSTERS
2 MEDIUM-SIZED CARROTS
16 MEDIUM-SIZED ASPARAGUS SPEARS, PENCIL SIZE
4 TEASPOONS UNSALTED BUTTER
½ POUND DRY ANGEL HAIR PASTA
KOSHER SALT AND WHITE PEPPER TO TASTE
2 TEASPOONS CHOPPED CHIVES
1 BATCH VANILLA BEURRE BLANC (RECIPE FOLLOWS)

1. In a large 9-quart stockpot with lid, boil 2 inches of water. At the boil, add the lobsters, and replace the lid. Cook the lobsters covered for 10 minutes. Remove the lobsters from the pot and place on a pan to cool. *Reserve the cooking liquid.* When the lobsters are cool enough to handle, remove the meat from the knuckles, claws and tail (discarding the vein). Cut off the tail fin to use as a garnish. Place the meat and the tail fins on an ovenproof pan or plate with sides just large enough to hold the meat in a single layer. Add ⅛ cup of the reserved cooking liquid to the pan with the meat and cover with foil. Reserve.

2. Peel the carrots and use a mandoline fit with a very fine blade to get a very thin carrot shred (julienne). If you don't have a mandoline, cut the carrots into 2-inch lengths, slice thinly (⅛ inch) lengthwise, stack a few slices and cut into long (⅛-inch) narrow strips. Remove the tough white lower sections from the asparagus spears. Peel the lower two to three inches of tough outer skin from the bottom of the asparagus. Blanch in a large pot of salted boiling water for about 1 minute and immediately place in a bowl of ice water to cool.

Vanilla may seem like an unusual companion for lobster at first, but once you taste sweet and succulent Maine lobster with this sauce, you will fully appreciate how dramatic this matching can be. ■

3. To serve, heat the oven to 350 degrees. Place the lobster (in prepared pans) in the oven for 20 minutes. Boil salted water in a large 4- or 5-quart saucepan for the pasta. Heat the carrots and asparagus in separate pans with 2 teaspoons of butter each. Season the vegetables with salt and white pepper. Add pasta to the boiling water and cook for 1 minute or until al dente. Strain the pasta well and place in a bowl. Add half of the Vanilla beurre blanc to the pasta and season with salt and white pepper. Cover to keep warm.

4. Remove the lobster meat from the oven. Make a small nest of pasta in the center of the plate. Fan four asparagus spears on the bottom of the plate (representing the legs of the lobsters). Place a small amount of the shredded carrots on the top of the plate.

5. To recreate the lobster, place the lobster tail on the pasta nest and fan out the reserved tail fin at the bottom of the tail. Place the knuckles (arm pieces) and claws on the plates, coming off the top part of the tail and pasta nest. Top the lobster meat with the remaining Vanilla beurre blanc and sprinkle with the chopped chives. Serve immediately.

BEURRE BLANC

4 TABLESPOONS UNSALTED BUTTER
1 TABLESPOON CANOLA OIL
1/4 CUP CHOPPED YELLOW ONION
1/2 CUP DRY WHITE WINE
2 TABLESPOONS WHITE WINE VINEGAR
1/2 SMALL BAY LEAF
1/2 CUP HEAVY CREAM
SALT AND WHITE PEPPER TO TASTE

1. Select a flavor variation from the list below and adapt those changes to this recipe.

2. Dice the butter and bring to room temperature.

3. Heat the oil in a small 2-quart saucepan. Sauté the onions over medium heat for 2 minutes but do not allow them to brown. Deglaze with the white wine and vinegar. Add the bay leaf and reduce over medium heat until most of the liquid has evaporated. Again, do not brown. Add the heavy cream and reduce the mixture by half, whisking occasionally.

4. Remove the pan from the heat and immediately whisk in the butter until well incorporated. Strain through a fine mesh strainer into a small bowl, discarding the solids. Season with salt and white pepper. Keep in a warm place (not too hot or it will break) until serving.

VANILLA: Add the seeds from $^1/_2$ vanilla bean (or $^1/_4$ teaspoon pure vanilla extract) to the sauce with the butter (cut the vanilla bean lengthwise and scrape out the tiny seeds with a paring knife)

LEMON: Add the juice and finely grated zest from $^1/_2$ lemon to the finished sauce

LEMON-CAPER: Add the juice and finely grated zest from $^1/_2$ lemon and 1 Tablespoon coarsely chopped capers to the finished sauce

BLUEBERRY: Add $^1/_4$ cup of fresh or frozen blueberries when deglazing with the white wine and vinegar in step 3 above

PASSION FRUIT: Heat 1 teaspoon unsalted butter in a small saucepan with a $^1/_4$ teaspoon ground annatto seeds over medium heat for 2 minutes; add the juice from 1 passion fruit or 1 Tablespoon passion fruit concentrate; whisk mixture into the sauce with the butter in step 4 above

Beurre Blanc is one of the most versatile sauces found on my menus. It goes well with many different types of food, including pasta, vegetables, fish, shellfish and light meats such as veal and chicken. A traditional beurre blanc does not have cream in it, but adding cream to this recipe helps stabilize the sauce and creates another depth of richness. The addition of various flavorings and garnishes can also dramatically change the character of the sauce. ■

Seared Maine Diver Scallops with Caribbean-Smoked Salmon and Sweet Potatoes

Maine diver scallops are available from December 1st to April 15th and are called diver scallops because they are actually hand harvested from the seabed by local divers. The result is a large fresh scallop that is rather sweet and delicious. The smoked salmon I use for this dish comes from my own on-property smoker and is cured with Caribbean spices. A good quality smoked salmon with a sprinkling of the spice mix is a good substitute.

■

SERVES 4

2 LARGE SWEET POTATOES
2 TEASPOONS EXTRA VIRGIN OLIVE OIL
KOSHER SALT AND BLACK PEPPER
2 TABLESPOONS UNSALTED BUTTER
2 TABLESPOONS BROWN SUGAR, FIRMLY PACKED
PINCH OF FRESHLY GRATED NUTMEG
8 OUNCES SLICED ATLANTIC SMOKED SALMON
20 LARGE DIVER SEA SCALLOPS, DRY
FOUR 10-INCH BAMBOO SKEWERS
3 TABLESPOONS CANOLA OIL
2 TEASPOONS Caribbean dry spice mix (RECIPE, PAGE 169)
PASSION FRUIT BEURRE BLANC (RECIPE, PAGE 133)
FENNEL AND ASPARAGUS SLAW (RECIPE FOLLOWS)

1. Preheat the oven to 400 degrees.

2. Cut the sweet potatoes in half lengthwise, brush with olive oil and season with kosher salt and black pepper. Place cut side down on a baking sheet and roast until tender, about 50 minutes, and cool slightly. Scoop the pulp out of the potato skins and into a small bowl. Discard the skins.

3. Add soft butter, brown sugar and freshly grated nutmeg to the potato pulp and mash well. Cover the bowl and keep warm.

4. Lay out the smoked salmon slices on a cutting board. Each scallop will be wrapped with a slice of smoked salmon, so 20 slices are needed. Slice some of

the larger salmon strips in half lengthwise, if needed.

5. Remove and discard the side muscle from the scallops and roll each scallop with a smoked salmon strip, following the curved contour of the scallop. Skewer the scallops, five to a skewer, securing the end of the smoked salmon strip and leaving a little space between each scallop. Place the skewers on a plate and drizzle with canola oil. Sprinkle with Caribbean dry spice mix and kosher salt and repeat with the oil, spice and salt on the other side. Let the skewers marinate for about 15 minutes, turning over halfway through.

6. In a large hot skillet or grill pan set over medium-high heat, sear the skewers for 3 minutes on each side or until cooked through. Remove the bamboo skewers.

7. To serve, place a small mound of the Fennel and asparagus slaw in the center of each plate. Place five dollops of the warm sweet potato puree evenly around the slaw mound on each plate. Top each dollop of sweet potato with a scallop. Drizzle a small pool of the Passion fruit beurre blanc next to each scallop and top the slaw with the reserved fennel sprigs.

FENNEL AND ASPARAGUS SLAW

1 BUNCH ASPARAGUS (1 POUND)
1 HEAD FRESH FENNEL
2 TABLESPOONS FINELY CHOPPED RED ONIONS
2 TABLESPOONS MINCED ITALIAN PARSLEY
1/2 CUP MAYONNAISE
1 TEASPOON DIJON MUSTARD
2 TABLESPOONS EXTRA VIRGIN OLIVE OIL
2 PINCHES FRESHLY GROUND BLACK PEPPER
1/4 TEASPOON CRUSHED FENNEL SEEDS, TOASTED
KOSHER SALT TO TASTE
4 SPRIGS FENNEL RESERVED FOR GARNISH

1. Boil 2 quarts of water in a 4-quart saucepan. Remove and discard the tough white lower sections from the asparagus spears. Peel the lower 2 to 3 inches of tough outer skin from the bottom of the remaining asparagus spears. Cut the asparagus spears on the bias into 1-inch pieces. Blanch in a large pot of salted boiling water for 1 minute and immediately place in a bowl of ice water to cool. Pat dry.

2. Cut the head of fennel in half lengthwise. Remove the tough core and any damaged outside layers. Thinly slice the fennel across the grain.

3. Combine all the ingredients in a bowl and mix well. Season with salt.

Sweet Potato–Crusted Salmon with a Blueberry Beurre Blanc

SERVES 4

1 SPAGHETTI SQUASH
2 CUPS SUGAR SNAP PEAS
3 TABLESPOONS UNSALTED BUTTER
FOUR 5-OUNCE SALMON FILLET PORTIONS, SKINLESS
    AND BONELESS
1 SWEET POTATO (8 OUNCES)
1 TABLESPOON ALL-PURPOSE FLOUR
1 LARGE EGG, LIGHTLY BEATEN
3 TABLESPOONS EXTRA VIRGIN OLIVE OIL
KOSHER SALT, WHITE PEPPER AND
    FRESHLY GROUND BLACK PEPPER TO TASTE
3 TABLESPOONS UNSALTED BUTTER
1 BATCH BLUEBERRY BEURRE BLANC (RECIPE, PAGE 133)
1/8 CUP FRESH BLUEBERRIES

With a last name of Salmon and an abundance of high-quality local fish by the same name, I had better be able to produce some unique dishes with this superior fish. The sweet potato combines so well with the salmon, forming a crisp crust with a little sweetness. The addition of wild Maine blueberries (much smaller and less sweet than those found in other areas of the country) adds a local twist to the dish while fully complementing the fish. ∎

1 TABLESPOON CHOPPED CHIVES
8 LONG CHIVE STEMS FOR GARNISH

1. Preheat the oven to 350 degrees. A typical small spaghetti squash weighs about $2^1/2$ pounds. Cut it in half lengthwise (only $^1/2$ is needed for this recipe) and prepare it by scooping out and discarding all the seeds, like you would a pumpkin. Place the spaghetti squash face down on a baking sheet with sides. Add water to cover the bottom of the pan to $^1/4$ inch and bake the squash in the center of the preheated oven for 40 minutes. Remove from the oven and let cool slightly. With a fork, gently scrape the flesh from the hard skin, discarding the skin. Reserve. Wash and trim the sugar snap peas, removing each end and pulling off any strings that extend the length of the pea.

2. Season four salmon portions with salt and white pepper. Peel and grate the sweet potato, using the coarse ($^1/4$-inch holes) side of a four-sided hand grater. Season the grated sweet potato with salt and white pepper. Flour the salmon, dusting off excess flour; brush the top only with the lightly beaten egg and coat with a layer of the grated sweet potato.

3. Heat a large sauté pan over medium-high heat and add 3 Tablespoons olive oil. Gently place the salmon fillets (coated side down) in the pan, being careful not to splash the hot oil. Sauté the salmon for 4 minutes on the first side, crisping the sweet potato crust to a golden brown. Gently flip the fillet and crisp the other side for 4 minutes. If the salmon fillet is thick, it may be necessary to continue the cooking process in a hot oven for a few minutes. It is very important not to overcook the salmon, as it will dry out. The flesh should just turn opaque and firm. Drain lightly on a paper towel to remove excess oil.

4. Just before serving, heat two small sauté pans over medium-high heat. Sauté the spaghetti squash in one pan with 2 Tablespoons butter and the sugar snap peas in the other pan with 1 Tablespoon butter. Cook the sugar snap peas for

1 minute, add a Tablespoon of water and continue cooking for 1 minute more. Cook the squash until heated through. Season both with salt and black pepper.

5. To serve, place a mound of spaghetti squash in the center of each plate. Top with the salmon and surround with a pool of the Blueberry beurre blanc. Place the sugar snap peas on each side of the salmon and sprinkle the plate with fresh blueberries and chopped chives. Cross two long chives over the salmon and serve.

HARTSTONE SMASHED POTATOES

SERVES 8

2 POUNDS LARGE RED POTATOES
1 TEASPOON SALT
3/4 CUP WHOLE MILK
1/4 CUP UNSALTED BUTTER
2 PINCHES WHITE PEPPER
SALT TO TASTE

1. Peel and cut the potatoes into 1/2-inch pieces. Place the potatoes in a 2-quart saucepan and cover with cold water by 1 inch and add salt. Cover and bring to a boil over high heat. Reduce to a simmer and cook for 30 minutes.

2. Drain off all the water and add the milk, butter and white pepper. Return the potatoes to the heat for 5 minutes to heat the milk. Remove from the heat and smash the potatoes, leaving them somewhat chunky. Add any additional flavoring if desired from the following variations and adjust the seasoning with salt. Keep covered for up to 30 minutes in a warm place before serving.

PARMESAN: Add 1/2 cup shredded Parmesan cheese

I have always preferred potatoes with a little more texture than those highly whipped fluffy ones that are so common. The term smashed comes from gently pressing on the potatoes with a potato masher, breaking up about half the chunks, leaving them a bit lumpy. Various seasonings and flavorings can really transform the potatoes into something exceptional. ■

GARLIC: Sauté 1 Tablespoon finely chopped garlic in 2 teaspoons olive oil over medium heat until golden brown

SCALLION OR CHIVE: Add 2 Tablespoons of either chopped scallions or chopped chives

PORTABELLA: Cut 2 large portabella mushroom caps into $^{1}/_{2}$-inch pieces and sauté in 2 Tablespoons unsalted butter over medium heat for 2 minutes

CARAMELIZED VIDALIA ONION: Peel 1 medium-sized Vidalia onion, cut in half from end to end and cut into thin strips from end to end; sauté in 2 teaspoons olive oil over medium heat until deep golden brown, stirring occasionally

ROASTED PEPPER: Add $^{1}/_{2}$ cup finely chopped roasted red bell pepper

Veal Saltimbocca

SERVES 4

FOUR 5-OUNCE VEAL CUTLETS
KOSHER SALT AND FRESHLY GROUND BLACK PEPPER TO TASTE
6 OUNCES THINLY SLICED PROSCIUTTO
6 OUNCES THINLY SLICED PROVOLONE OR FONTINA CHEESE
10 FRESH SAGE LEAVES
2 TABLESPOONS OLIVE OIL
$^{1}/_{4}$ CUP ALL-PURPOSE FLOUR
1 BATCH BEURRE BLANC (RECIPE, PAGE 132)
1 TEASPOON COARSELY CHOPPED ITALIAN PARSLEY
$^{1}/_{2}$ BATCH HARTSTONE SMASHED POTATOES (RECIPE, PAGE 139)
SEASONAL VEGETABLES OF YOUR CHOICE

1. Place a veal cutlet between two 12-inch pieces of plastic wrap. Gently pound out

Turkey or chicken breast can be easily substituted for the veal cutlets if desired. Trim any excess fat or cartilage from a 5-ounce boneless and skinless chicken breast. If the breast is thick, you may want to butter-fly it by laying it flat on the cutting board, and thinly slicing the breast in half, stopping short of separating the two halves. Fold the breast open and pound out between plastic as instructed for the veal. For turkey breast, simply slice 5-ounce cutlets from a raw and skinless turkey breast. ■

the veal to about $1/8$-inch thick with a meat mallet. Be careful not to rip holes into the veal by pounding it too thin in areas. Continue with the remaining cutlets.

2. Remove the top sheet of plastic from the cutlets and season with salt and pepper. Divide the prosciutto and provolone or fontina cheese into 6 stacks, reserving 2 stacks for garnish. Top the remaining 4 stacks with a whole sage leaf. Place the stacks over half of each pounded veal cutlet, leaving a $1/2$-inch strip of veal exposed around the edge. Fold the empty half of the veal over the prosciutto and cheese, making sure that the top reaches the exposed veal edge along the bottom. With the back of a large knife, gently press the edges of the veal pouch to seal the edges. *The veal can be prepared to this stage hours in advance, covered and refrigerated until just before serving.*

3. Shortly before serving, prepare the Beurre blanc. Finely slice 2 whole sage leaves and stir into the Beurre blanc. Keep in a warm place until serving. Finely slice the reserved 2 stacks of prosciutto and cheese, and with your fingertips, gently mix together. Reserve until serving.

4. Heat the olive oil in a large sauté pan over medium-high heat. Lightly coat each side of the veal with flour, shaking off the excess. When the oil is hot, place the stuffed veal pouches in the sauté pan. Cook until lightly browned on the first side, about 3 minutes, and then gently flip over with a spatula and lightly brown for another 3 minutes on the other side.

5. To serve, place the veal on the plate and ladle some of the Beurre blanc on top. Place $1/4$ of the sliced prosciutto and cheese on top of the veal in a small mound. Sprinkle with the chopped parsley and garnish with a fresh sage leaf.

6. Serve with Hartstone smashed potatoes and seasonal vegetables of your choice.

PLANTAIN-CRUSTED HALIBUT WITH MAINE CRABMEAT

SERVES 4

FOUR 6-OUNCE HALIBUT FILLETS
1/2 POUND MAINE CRABMEAT
2 TABLESPOONS MAYONNAISE
1 SCALLION, GREEN PART ONLY, MINCED
2 TEASPOONS MINCED RED BELL PEPPER
KOSHER SALT AND BLACK PEPPER TO TASTE
2 TABLESPOONS ALL-PURPOSE FLOUR
1 LARGE EGG, WHISKED IN A SMALL BOWL
3 OUNCES PLANTAIN CHIPS, GROUND IN A
    FOOD PROCESSOR TO THE SIZE OF OATMEAL
3 TABLESPOONS CANOLA OIL

LEMON BEURRE BLANC (RECIPE, PAGE 133)
LEMON SEGMENTS AND ITALIAN PARSLEY LEAVES FOR GARNISH
SEASONAL VEGETABLES OF YOUR CHOICE

1. Slice the halibut fillets in half and pound gently between two pieces of plastic wrap to about 1/4-inch thick.

2. Mix crabmeat with mayonnaise, scallion, red pepper, and season with salt and pepper.

3. Lay the pounded halibut out on the counter and divide the crabmeat mixture between 4 of the halibut pieces. Spread the mixture on each, leaving half an inch of the halibut exposed along the edges. Top the crab mixture with the

other 4 pieces of halibut, then use the back of a knife to gently press the two edges together on each of the 4 servings.

4. Season the halibut pouches with salt and pepper and dust with flour. Dip the halibut into the egg mixture and coat both sides. Then dip into the ground plantain chips to coat each side.

5. Sauté the halibut in canola oil, over medium heat for 3 minutes, and then gently flip over with a spatula and cook for 3 minutes on the other side. Drain on paper towels.

6. Serve the halibut over a pool of Lemon beurre blanc and garnish with the Italian parsley leaves and lemon segments. Serve with seasonal vegetables.

PAN-SEARED DUCK BREAST WITH A BERRY-CITRUS BORDELAISE

SERVES 4

4 DUCK BREASTS (MAPLE LEAF FARMS IS A GREAT BRAND)
1 TABLESPOON CANOLA OIL
1 1/2 TEASPOONS HERBES DE PROVENCE
1 TEASPOON KOSHER SALT
FRESHLY GROUND BLACK PEPPER

1 CUP FRESH OR FROZEN BERRIES
    (ANY BERRY OR COMBINATION OF BERRIES YOU LIKE)
2 TEASPOONS CHAMBORD (RASPBERRY LIQUEUR)
2 TABLESPOONS ORANGE JUICE
1 TEASPOON LIME JUICE
1 CUP BORDELAISE (RECIPE FOLLOWS)
1/2 BATCH HARTSTONE SMASHED POTATOES (RECIPE, PAGE 139)

For consistent and flavorful duck breasts I use Maple Leaf Farms brand duck products. They raise and sell White Pekin ducklings, which are "Long Island style" ducklings. Check out their Web site at www.mapleleaffarms.com for a supplier near you, for more information about their products or to order their products online. ■

ADDITIONAL FRESH BERRIES, CITRUS ZEST AND CHOPPED
ITALIAN PARSLEY FOR GARNISH
SEASONAL VEGETABLES OF YOUR CHOICE

1. Trim any excess skin, fat and silver-skin from the duck breast. I like to remove any skin that extends over the top surface of the duck breast. Rub both sides of the duck breast with the oil and coat both sides with the herbes de Provence, salt and black pepper. Allow the duck to marinate for 1 hour.

2. Combine the berries, Chambord, orange juice, lime juice and Bordelaise in a small saucepan. Place the pan over medium heat and simmer the sauce for 10 minutes. Pass the sauce through a fine strainer, pressing all of the juices out of the berries. Keep warm and covered until serving.

3. Preheat the oven to 350 degrees.

4. Place a large sauté pan over high heat until it is very hot. Place the duck breasts in the pan, skin side down, and reduce the heat to medium-high. Continue cooking for 5 minutes on the first side. Turn the breasts over and sear the second side for 5 minutes. Remove the duck to an ovenproof pan and place in the oven to finish cooking for 5–7 minutes.

5. Remove the duck from the oven and let stand 3 minutes to allow the juices to settle. Arrange potatoes and vegetables of your choice on the serving plates. Slice each duck breast on a bias into about 6 slices. Fan out the sliced breast on the plates and ladle some of the sauce in front. Garnish with fresh berries, citrus zest and chopped parsley.

BORDELAISE

MAKES 2½ CUPS

3 TABLESPOONS UNSALTED BUTTER
1 SHALLOT, MINCED
3 TABLESPOONS ALL-PURPOSE FLOUR
1 CUP DRY RED WINE
½ SMALL BAY LEAF
1 SPRIG FRESH THYME
10 BLACK PEPPERCORNS, CRACKED
2 CUPS BROWN VEAL STOCK (RECIPE BELOW)
SALT TO TASTE

1. Heat a 2-quart saucepan over medium heat. Add the butter to the pan and then the minced shallot. Stir for 1 minute and add the flour. Cook, stirring for 2 minutes.

2. Add the red wine, bay leaf, thyme, peppercorns and veal stock and bring to a boil. Reduce the heat to low and simmer for 15 minutes.

3. Season to taste with salt, then strain through a fine mesh strainer. *Bordelaise will keep for 1 week covered in the refrigerator and freezes well for up to 3 months.*

BROWN VEAL STOCK

10 POUNDS VEAL BONES (A COMBINATION OF MEATY
   BREAST BONES AND GELATINOUS LARGE BONES WORKS WELL)
2 TABLESPOONS CANOLA OIL
1 POUND YELLOW ONIONS
1 POUND CARROTS

Making stocks and sauces is a time-consuming process, but it is also very rewarding. If you can't find the time to make your own bordelaise from scratch, I have a wonderful bordelaise base available for sale on my Web site, and your sauce can be completed in minutes. To crack peppercorns, simply place whole peppercorns on a cutting board and rock a heavy saucepan back and forth on top of them, cracking them into random-sized pieces. ■

3 STALKS CELERY

¼ CUP TOMATO PASTE

2 CUPS DRY RED WINE

1 BAY LEAF

2 FRESH THYME SPRIGS

1 TEASPOON BLACK PEPPERCORNS

1. Preheat the oven to 450 degrees.

2. Coat the bottom of two roasting pans with the canola oil and divide the veal bones between the two pans. Place the pans in the hot oven and roast for 30 minutes, browning the bones well.

3. Roughly cut the onions, carrots and celery into 1-inch pieces. Add the vegetables to the browned bones and roast for another 15 minutes.

4. Brush the bones with the tomato paste and return to the oven for 10 more minutes.

5. Empty the contents of the roasting pans into a 14-quart (or larger) stockpot. Place the roasting pans on the stove over medium heat and divide the wine between the two pans. Deglaze the pans by scraping all the fond (brown cooked-on bits) from the bottom of the pans with a metal spatula. Use additional water if necessary to clean all fond from the pan. Place all of these juices into the pot with the bones and vegetables. Cover the bones with about 2 gallons of water and add the bay leaf, fresh thyme and peppercorns. Place the stockpot over high heat and bring to a boil. Reduce the heat to low, and simmer the stock for 12 hours.

6. Strain the stock through a fine strainer and discard all the solids. Skim off any visible fat.

7. The next step is reducing the stock. I like to take a large saucepan (4-quart) and fill it with the stock. Bring to a boil over high heat and reduce to a high

simmer. Skim and discard any impurities or fat from the surface of the stock during this stage. As the stock reduces, replenish with the remaining stock until it has all been added and has further reduced to about 3 quarts.

8. It is important to cool the reduced stock to room temperature before you place it in the refrigerator. This can be done many different ways: divide the stock into shallow containers to cool, immerse a pot of the strained stock into a sink full of ice water or set the pot in a snow bank outside the kitchen door. Once the stock has cooled, refrigerate it in a covered container. The stock will gel up firm after it has cooled. *Stock will keep up to 1 week in the refrigerator or can be frozen in freezer bags or small covered containers for up to 3 months.*

The Mushroom Hunter

LIKE MANY MAINERS, Mark DiGirolamo has a job description that changes with the seasons. During the summer, he runs Breakwater Kayak Company out of Rockland Harbor; the rest of the year, he teaches science in the alternative education program at Camden Hills Regional High School. But what really makes DiGirolamo's heart sing is the time he spends on the hunt for wild mushrooms. From July through October, he searches under oak trees and conifers for chanterelles, porcini and oyster mushrooms that grow wild in the woods of Maine. Distinguishing edible wild mushrooms from their inedible cousins is not a task for the fainthearted.

The catalyst for DiGirolamo was a dish his Italian grandmother called "nasce"—wild marinated mushrooms that appeared on her Sunday dinner table every fall. It took years of tramping through the woods, consulting field guides and discussing this mysterious mushroom with more experienced foragers before he discovered the English name and appearance of the fungi he had only ever seen marinated. Today, "hen of the woods" appears on the menu at the Hartstone Inn only when DiGirolamo has gathered enough to satisfy his own craving first.

Wild Mushroom Risotto

*Mushroom risotto is a very hearty dish—great for a chilly, fall evening. A small portion of the risotto works well as an appetizer or you can enjoy it as your main course. I prefer the combination of dried and fresh mushrooms to introduce more flavors to the dish, and if you can get your hands on some fresh wild mushrooms, it is well worth the effort and money. Arborio is a short-*and fat-grain, Italian-grown rice that is ideal for risotto because it absorbs the flavors of the dish, maintains its texture and produces the creaminess that risotto is known for.* ■

SERVES 4

2 OUNCES DRIED WILD MUSHROOMS
  (PORCINI, OYSTER, CHANTERELLES, MORELS, ETC.)
3 TABLESPOONS EXTRA VIRGIN OLIVE OIL
1/4 POUND PANCETTA
3 CUPS CHICKEN STOCK
3 TABLESPOONS UNSALTED BUTTER
1 CUP FINELY CHOPPED YELLOW ONION
4 CLOVES GARLIC, MINCED
1/2 POUND FRESH WILD MUSHROOMS (PORCINI, OYSTER,
  CHANTERELLES, MORELS, ETC.) OR USE PORTABELLA
  MUSHROOMS, ROUGHLY CUT INTO 1/2-INCH PIECES,
  RESERVING A FEW SLICES FOR GARNISH
1/2 CUP UNSALTED BUTTER
2 CUPS ARBORIO RICE
1/2 TEASPOON FRESH THYME
1/2 TEASPOON OREGANO
1 CUP DRY RED WINE
1/2 CUP HEAVY CREAM
1/2 CUP PARMESAN CHEESE, GRATED
SALT AND FRESHLY GROUND BLACK PEPPER TO TASTE
1 TABLESPOON COARSELY CHOPPED ITALIAN PARSLEY
4 SPRIGS FRESH THYME FOR GARNISH

1. Place the dried mushrooms in a medium-sized bowl and cover with 2 cups warm water. Let the mushrooms sit in the water for 1 hour. Drain off the liquid, adding it to the chicken stock, and cut the mushrooms into 1/2-inch pieces. Reserve.

2. Heat the olive oil in a 4-quart saucepan over medium heat. Dice the pancetta into ¼-inch cubes, and cook gently in the olive oil (stirring often) until golden brown and crisp. With a slotted spoon, remove the pancetta from the pan and reserve, leaving the fat in the saucepan.

3. Bring the chicken stock to a simmer in another saucepan.

4. Add the butter to the saucepan used for the pancetta. When it has melted, add the onion and cook for 3 minutes. Add the garlic and stir, cooking for 30 seconds. Stir in the fresh and dry mushrooms and cook for 2 minutes, stirring occasionally. Pour the contents of the pan into a strainer set over a small bowl (to collect the juices).

5. Return the pan to the heat and add the ½ cup butter. Melt, and add the Arborio rice, thyme and oregano. Stir, over medium heat, for 4 minutes, lightly toasting the rice. Add the red wine and cook until dry. Add 1 cup of the hot chicken stock and continue to cook the rice, stirring often. When the rice has absorbed the first cup of stock, continue by adding 1 cup of hot stock at a time, allowing the rice to absorb the stock each time before adding more. Continue until the rice is just tender, with a little crispness, about 30 minutes.

6. When the rice is done, stir in the cooked mushrooms, heavy cream, pancetta and all but 1 Tablespoon of the Parmesan cheese. Mix well. Adjust the seasoning with salt and black pepper.

7. To serve, divide the risotto between 4 serving plates. Top with the reserved sliced mushrooms, the 1 Tablespoon Parmesan cheese, chopped Italian parsley and fresh thyme sprigs.

Cajun-Seared Tenderloin of Beef with Oven-Roasted Tomatoes and Bleu Cheese

My Cajun spice mix is very easy to make and goes well with any meat or fish dish where you want to introduce that "Bayou" flavor. Oven drying tomatoes is a terrific way to intensify the flavors and texture of a ripe tomato. I also smoke/dry tomatoes, which adds another layer of flavor and goes well with this dish. The combination of the Cajun spice on the beef, oven-dried tomatoes, red onions and the bleu cheese is quite spectacular. ■

SERVES 4

6 PLUM TOMATOES
2 TABLESPOONS EXTRA VIRGIN OLIVE OIL
KOSHER SALT AND FRESHLY GROUND BLACK PEPPER TO TASTE
FOUR 6-OUNCE BEEF FILETS
2 TABLESPOONS OLIVE OIL
4 TEASPOONS CAJUN SPICE MIX (RECIPE FOLLOWS)
1 TEASPOON KOSHER SALT
1 TABLESPOON UNSALTED BUTTER
1 SMALL RED ONION, SLICED THINLY

1/2 BATCH HARTSTONE SMASHED POTATOES (RECIPE, PAGE 139)
1 CUP BORDELAISE (RECIPE, PAGE 145)
SEASONAL VEGETABLES OF YOUR CHOICE
3 OUNCES BLEU CHEESE (GOOD QUALITY CHEESE LIKE STILTON, GORGONZOLA OR DANISH BLEU CASTELLO), CRUMBLED
3 TABLESPOONS OF YOUR FAVORITE BLEU CHEESE DRESSING
1 TEASPOON COARSELY CHOPPED ITALIAN PARSLEY

1. Preheat the oven to 375 degrees. Line a baking sheet with parchment paper and brush the paper with 1 teaspoon of the olive oil.

2. Cut the plum tomatoes in half lengthwise and place them cut side up on the baking sheet. Drizzle the tomatoes with the remainder of the 2 Tablespoons of olive oil and sprinkle the tomatoes with kosher salt and freshly ground black pepper. Bake in the preheated oven for 2 hours.

3. Place the beef filets on a plate and coat on both sides with olive oil. Coat all around with Cajun spice mix and kosher salt. Marinate the beef in the refrigerator for 1 hour.

4. Heat a large sauté pan over medium-high heat. When the pan is very hot, sear the beef filets for 4 minutes. Turn the filets over and sear on the other side for 4 minutes. Depending on how you like your beef cooked, it may be necessary to preheat an oven and finish the beef in the oven. Cook it to your preference.

5. Heat a medium-sized sauté pan over medium-high heat and melt the butter. Add the sliced red onions and cook, stirring for 2 minutes. Season with salt and black pepper.

6. Place a scoop of Hartstone smashed potatoes on the plates and top with the seared beef filet. Place seasonal vegetables of your choice on the back of the plate, and ladle the heated Bordelaise on the front of the plate. Top the beef with an oven-roasted tomato half, and place two more halves in the Bordelaise. Top the beef with the crumbled bleu cheese, the sautéed onion and drizzle with the bleu cheese dressing. Sprinkle with Italian parsley and serve.

CAJUN SPICE MIX

1/4 CUP KOSHER SALT

1/4 CUP GROUND SWEET PAPRIKA

3 TABLESPOONS GROUND CAYENNE PEPPER

2 TABLESPOONS FRESHLY GROUND BLACK PEPPER

2 TABLESPOONS DRIED THYME LEAVES

2 TABLESPOONS CELERY SEED

2 TABLESPOONS DRIED OREGANO

2 TABLESPOONS ONION POWDER

2 TABLESPOONS GARLIC POWDER

2 TABLESPOONS GRANULATED SUGAR

2 TEASPOONS DRIED BASIL

1 TEASPOON CHILI POWDER
1/2 TEASPOON GROUND CUMIN
1/2 TEASPOON GROUND CORIANDER

1. Mix all the spices and dried herbs together and keep in a covered jar.

Olive-Encrusted Rack of Lamb with a Rosemary Bordelaise

SERVES 4

4 FULL RACKS OF NEW ZEALAND LAMB, FRENCHED
2 TABLESPOONS OLIVE OIL
1 TABLESPOON MINCED GARLIC
2 TEASPOONS MINCED FRESH ROSEMARY
KOSHER SALT AND FRESHLY GROUND BLACK PEPPER
4 TABLESPOONS OLIVE OIL
1 CUP MIXED OLIVES (OR OLIVES OF YOUR CHOICE), PITTED
1/3 CUP PANKO BREAD CRUMBS

1 CUP BORDELAISE (RECIPE, PAGE 145)
1 TEASPOON MINCED FRESH ROSEMARY
1/2 BATCH HARTSTONE SMASHED POTATOES (RECIPE, PAGE 139)
SEASONAL VEGETABLES OF YOUR CHOICE
4 SPRIGS FRESH ROSEMARY AND 12 WHOLE PITTED OLIVES
     FOR GARNISH

Ask your butcher to French the lamb racks for you. A Frenched lamb rack has the meat scraped off the rib bones, exposing the clean bones, which creates a cleaner and more stunning presentation. I have always been an olive fanatic and love the combination of lamb with olives. An olive tapenade works great in this dish in place of the olive puree. ∎

1. Cut each lamb rack in half, cutting between the bones. Rub the lamb with the 2 Tablespoons olive oil, garlic, 2 teaspoons minced rosemary, kosher salt and black pepper. Let marinate 1 hour.

2. Preheat the oven to 350 degrees.

3. Place olives in the bowl of a food processor (check twice for pits) and process until it is relatively smooth. Reserve.

4. Heat a large sauté pan over medium heat. Add the 4 Tablespoons olive oil and sear the seasoned lamb racks for 3 minutes on each side. Turn the lamb racks so that the meat side is up and spread evenly with the olive paste. Sprinkle the panko breadcrumbs over the olive paste. Lightly pat the breadcrumbs to adhere them to the olive paste.

5. Place the lamb (olive crust up) on a baking sheet and roast in the oven for about 25 minutes (depending on the size of the lamb) for medium, or longer, if desired.

6. Heat the Bordelaise and add 1 teaspoon minced rosemary.

7. To serve, place a scoop of Hartstone smashed potatoes in the center of each plate. Take 2 half racks per plate and face their bones to one another over the potatoes. Intertwine the bones to get them to stand up. Ladle a pool of Bordelaise on each side of the plate and fill the remaining plate with seasonal vegetables of your choice.

8. Garnish with fresh rosemary sprigs and whole pitted olives.

H

Desserts

# SOUFFLÉ

SERVES 10

2 CUPS WHOLE MILK
1/4 POUND UNSALTED BUTTER (1 STICK)
1 CUP ALL-PURPOSE FLOUR
1 CUP GRANULATED SUGAR
9 LARGE EGGS, SEPARATED
2 TABLESPOONS UNSALTED BUTTER, SOFT
3 TABLESPOONS GRANULATED SUGAR
1/2 TEASPOON CREAM OF TARTAR
FLAVORED CRÈME ANGLAISE (RECIPE, PAGE 55)

1. Heat the milk over medium heat, in a 2-quart saucepan. In another 2-quart saucepan, melt the butter over medium heat. When the butter is melted, stir in the flour and mix until combined well. Reduce heat to low, and stir frequently.

2. When the milk comes to a simmer, stir in the sugar. Continue to stir, dissolving the sugar for 2 minutes. Pour the milk mixture into the butter mixture and stir with a whisk to combine, cooking over medium heat until a ball forms and the mixture releases from the sides of the pan.

3. Immediately place the mixture in a mixing bowl and stir (using the flat paddle) on medium-low speed with an electric mixer for 10 minutes to cool.

4. One by one, stir in the egg yolks, allowing each to be completely incorporated before adding the next. When all of the egg yolks are incorporated, set the mixture (soufflé base) aside and allow it to cool. *This base will keep refrigerated for up to 1 week.*

5. Generously butter ten 1 1/2 cup soufflé dishes, covering the entire surface area

Soufflés have become my signature dessert at the Inn and guests always ask me for the recipe or a cooking class on soufflés. Making them can be tricky, so follow the instructions carefully. Timing is the key to successful soufflé serving, as they wait for no one. When they are ready to be served, they must be hastily escorted to the table and consumed immediately or they will become, as Mary Jo puts it, "flat tires." ■

on the inside of the cups, including the rim. Coat the buttered cups with granulated sugar, rotating the cups to coat them evenly. Tap out any excess sugar. Set the prepared cups aside.

6. Choose from the soufflé flavors below, and stir the ingredients into the base, mixing well.

GRAND MARNIER: $^1/_4$ cup Grand Marnier

CHOCOLATE-AMARETTO: $^1/_4$ cup cocoa powder, $^1/_4$ cup Amaretto and 2 Tablespoons finely ground almonds

RASPBERRY-CHAMBORD: $^1/_2$ cup fresh or individually quick frozen (IQF) raspberries and $^1/_4$ cup Chambord

CAPPUCCINO: 2 Tablespoons strong coffee or espresso and $^1/_4$ cup Kahlua

BLUEBERRY-HAZELNUT: $^1/_2$ cup fresh or frozen blueberries, $^1/_4$ cup Frangelico (hazelnut liqueur) and 2 Tablespoons finely ground hazelnuts

PISTACHIO: $^1/_4$ cup finely ground pistachios and 2 Tablespoons Amaretto

7. Preheat the oven to 350 degrees.

8. In an electric mixer fitted with a whisk, whip the egg whites and cream of tartar to stiff peaks. With a large rubber spatula, gently fold half of the egg whites into the base. Continue folding in the remaining egg whites. Gently pour the batter into the prepared soufflé dishes, filling them $^4/_5$ of the way full. *Be careful not to drip the batter on the rims, or the soufflés may not rise evenly.*

9. Bake in the center of a 350-degree oven for 35 minutes, or until lightly browned on top. Remove from the oven, place on a small serving plate and dust with powdered sugar. Hurry the soufflés to the table. The soufflés can be further garnished with the ingredients used to flavor the base (chopped nuts, cocoa powder, chocolate-covered coffee beans, etc.). Serve the soufflés with a

side of Crème anglaise, flavored to accompany your soufflé. Pour the Crème anglaise into a hole you poke in the top of the soufflé at the table. Eat immediately.

Tarte Tatin of Pears

2/3 CUP GRANULATED SUGAR
3 TABLESPOONS UNSALTED BUTTER
1 CUP PECAN PIECES
6 BOSC PEARS, FIRM AND RIPE
2 TEASPOONS BRANDY
1 SHEET PUFF PASTRY (HOMEMADE OR YOUR FAVORITE BRAND)

1. In a small saucepan, combine the sugar and butter. Cook over medium heat for about 15 minutes, until the sugar caramelizes to a dark amber color. Pour the caramel into the bottom of a 9-inch glass pie dish, covering as much of the bottom as possible. Sprinkle the pecan pieces over the caramel.

2. Preheat the oven to 400 degrees.

3. Peel the pears, cut them in half lengthwise and remove the core and stem with a melon baller. Cut each half in half again. Arrange half of the pear quarters, rounded side down, and points to the center, in a circle over the caramel. Arrange the remaining pears rounded side up, and points to the center, between the pears of the bottom layer, filling the gaps. Sprinkle the pears with the brandy.

4. Cut the puff pastry sheet into a 12-inch round circle, rolling it out if necessary. Place the pastry on top of the pears, tucking the excess in around the edges of the pears. Place on a center rack in the oven and bake for 55 minutes.

A tarte tatin is an upside-down tart, traditionally made with apples. It is named after two French sisters who created the dish in the Loire valley of France. My version is made with pecans and pears, but apples can be substituted if desired. Tarte Tatin is at its best when it comes directly from the oven, as the crust tends to get soggy from the caramel sauce.

5. Remove the tarte from the oven and let cool for 5 minutes. Place the serving platter over the top of the pie dish, and using a towel or potholder, invert the tarte quickly onto the platter. Cut into wedges and serve warm with vanilla ice cream.

BLUEBERRY-VANILLA CRÈME BRÛLÉE

SERVES 4

5 EGG YOLKS
1/4 CUP, PLUS 1 TEASPOON GRANULATED SUGAR
1/2 VANILLA BEAN, SEEDS SCRAPED OUT TO USE, POD
    RESERVED FOR ANOTHER USE (OR 1 TEASPOON
    VANILLA EXTRACT)
1 CUP HEAVY CREAM
3 TABLESPOONS WHOLE MILK
1/2 CUP FRESH OR FROZEN BLUEBERRIES
1/4 CUP PECAN PIECES (OPTIONAL)
WHIPPED CREAM
ADDITIONAL BLUEBERRIES AND 4 SPRIGS OF SPEARMINT
    FOR GARNISH

1. Preheat the oven to 325 degrees. Heat about 1 quart of water in a teakettle (or saucepan) for a hot water bath.

2. In a medium-sized bowl, whisk together the egg yolks and sugar. Add the vanilla and whisk in cream and milk.

3. Divide the blueberries and pecans between four shallow 3/4-cup volume ceramic dishes. Divide the custard mixture between the four dishes and place in a pan with at least 1-inch sides. Fill the pan with the hot water about halfway up the sides of the dishes.

Crème brûlée literally translates to "burnt cream," which refers to the crunchy layer of caramel that floats over the creamy and smooth custard below. Many of the specialty cooking supply stores carry a small butane torch that can be used for caramelizing the sugar on the surface of the crème brûlée. Another option is to dig around in your basement to find a propane torch used for plumbing projects. Either piece of equipment works well. ∎

4. Bake in the preheated oven for 40 minutes or until firm. Remove from the oven and water bath and cool. Refrigerate for at least 2 hours.

5. To serve, evenly sprinkle the top of each crème brûlée with enough granulated sugar to cover. Using a torch, slowly begin to caramelize the sugar, moving the torch around a lot to prevent burning in any given area. Serve with a dollop of whipped cream, some fresh blueberries and a sprig of fresh spearmint.

STICKY TOFFEE PUDDING

SERVES 9

2 CUPS PITTED AND CHOPPED DATES (11 OUNCES)
1½ TEASPOONS BAKING SODA
1½ CUPS BOILING WATER
2 TABLESPOONS RUM
¼ TEASPOON VANILLA
1 CUP GRANULATED SUGAR
½ CUP UNSALTED BUTTER, SOFT
2 LARGE EGGS
1½ CUPS ALL-PURPOSE FLOUR
1 BATCH CARAMEL-RUM SAUCE (RECIPE FOLLOWS)
VANILLA ICE CREAM
WHIPPED CREAM

1. Preheat the oven to 350 degrees. Butter and flour an 8-inch by 8-inch baking pan.

2. Combine the chopped dates and baking soda together in a small mixing bowl. Cover with boiling water, rum and vanilla and let set for 5 minutes.

3. In another bowl, cream together the sugar and butter. Add the eggs and mix well. Add flour and date mixture and stir until well incorporated.

A pub meal in England is not complete without a rich date pudding to finish off the meal. Sticky Toffee Pudding is, hands down, one of my all-time favorite desserts. The pudding and Caramel-rum sauce can be made well in advance and reheated just before serving. Top it with a premium vanilla ice cream and some whipped cream and you are in heaven. ■

4. Pour into the prepared baking pan and place in the center of the preheated oven. Bake for about 1 hour, or until a toothpick comes out clean. Let cool 5 minutes.

5. To serve, cut the pudding into 9 pieces (3 by 3) and serve drenched in Caramel-rum sauce with vanilla ice cream and whipped cream on top.

CARAMEL-RUM SAUCE

> 2 CUPS BROWN SUGAR, FIRMLY PACKED
> 1 CUP UNSALTED BUTTER
> 1/2 CUP DARK RUM
> 1 CUP HEAVY CREAM
> 2 TEASPOONS VANILLA EXTRACT

1. Bring all the ingredients, except the vanilla, to a boil in a small saucepan, stirring occasionally. Reduce the heat to low and simmer the sauce for 15 minutes over low heat. Stir in vanilla and keep warm until serving.

PISTACHIO AND CHOCOLATE GANACHE TART

> 1 BATCH PISTACHIO BROWNIES (RECIPE FOLLOWS)
> 1 POUND DARK (SWEETENED) CHOCOLATE, FINELY GRATED
> 1 1/2 CUPS HEAVY CREAM
> 2 OUNCES BAILEY'S IRISH CREAM
> 1 OUNCE GRAND MARNIER
> 1 TABLESPOON UNSALTED BUTTER
> 1 TEASPOON VANILLA EXTRACT
> CHOCOLATE ICE CREAM
> CHOCOLATE SAUCE

Chocolate lovers beware. Starting with a pistachio brownie crust and followed by a layer of rich chocolate ganache, chocolate ice cream and finally chocolate sauce, any chocoholic would be impressed. To hasten the process, a good-quality boxed fudge-brownie mix can be used with the addition of pistachios.

■

CARAMEL-RUM SAUCE (RECIPE, PAGE 161)
FRESHLY CHOPPED PISTACHIOS FOR GARNISH

1. Prepare the brownies and cool slightly.

2. Lightly butter a 9-inch tart pan with a removable bottom. Remove two-thirds of the brownies from the pan (the remaining third can be eaten as brownies) and press into the tart mold, evenly distributing it on the bottom and 1 inch up the sides.

3. Bring to a simmer 1 inch of water in a medium-sized saucepan. Combine the dark chocolate, heavy cream, Bailey's Irish Cream, Grand Marnier, butter and vanilla extract in a medium-sized mixing bowl, and place the bowl over the simmering water. Stir occasionally, until the chocolate melts and the mixture becomes smooth.

4. Pour the ganache into the brownie shell and chill for 2 hours or until it is firmly set up. Put the chocolate sauce and the Caramel-rum sauce in separate squirt bottles.

5. To serve, remove the tart from the refrigerator and using either a torch or the open flame from a gas range, warm the sides slightly to release the tart. Using a long thin knife dipped in hot water, cleaned and dried between slices, slice the tart into 12 wedges. On a plate, set a wedge of the tart and a scoop of chocolate ice cream on the side. Squirt chocolate sauce and Caramel-rum sauce over the tart, ice cream and plate. Sprinkle with chopped pistachios and serve immediately.

Pistachio Brownies

½ POUND DARK (SWEETENED) CHOCOLATE, FINELY GRATED
1 CUP UNSALTED BUTTER, CUT INTO SMALL PIECES
¼ CUP COCOA POWDER
½ CUP ALL-PURPOSE FLOUR
1 CUP GRANULATED SUGAR
¼ TEASPOON SALT
4 LARGE EGGS
1 TEASPOON VANILLA EXTRACT
1 TEASPOON PISTACHIO OR ALMOND EXTRACT
1 CUP SHELLED PISTACHIO NUTS, COARSELY CHOPPED

1. Preheat the oven to 350 degrees.

2. Butter and flour a 9-inch by 9-inch baking pan, tapping out the excess flour.

3. Bring to a simmer 1 inch of water in a medium-sized saucepan. Combine the grated chocolate and butter in a medium-sized mixing bowl, and place the bowl over the simmering water. Stir occasionally, until the mixture becomes smooth.

4. In another bowl, mix together the cocoa powder, flour, sugar and salt. Whisk in the eggs and extracts until the mixture is combined. Add this mixture to the melted chocolate and butter, and whisk together until smooth. Stir in the chopped pistachios.

5. Pour the brownie batter into the prepared baking pan and place in the center of the preheated 350-degree oven. Bake for 45 minutes and remove to a rack to cool.

ℋ

Cooking Classes

THE COOKING CLASSES I offer on Saturdays during Camden's off-season, November through April, give me a chance to share my kitchen and my knowledge of—and appreciation for—international cuisine. For students, the classes are a glimpse into my world as a restaurant chef, as well as an opportunity to learn knife techniques, where to buy ingredients for ethnic foods and, best of all, how to prepare several recipes from a particular tradition. The two-hour classes, held in the early afternoon, are limited to around 10 participants. A few students who have become regulars enjoy the experience so much that they schedule a private class for their entire family every year around the holidays.

I offer a range of cooking classes, including Haute Chinese, Maine seafood with Caribbean accents, Dim Sum, Thai, etc. Students sample wines specific to the region being taught that day, and while hands-on class participation is not mandatory, those who want to get involved are encouraged to. Toward the end of the class, four to eight dishes will have been prepared. (A word to the wise: Have a light lunch, if indeed you eat at all. Someone has to eat all the food you've helped cook.)

Though tackling a Thai meal, for example, may initially feel overwhelming, after 2 hours in the kitchen with me, many of my students will cook the meals again in their own homes and invite friends over to enjoy their accomplishment. Students walk away from each of the cooking classes with more confidence, copies of my recipes and possibly a list of must-haves for their kitchens after having seen what a microplane or a mandoline, for example, can do.

H

Caribbean Cuisine

ONE OF THE CUISINES closest to my heart is that of the Caribbean. I spent three years working on the Caribbean island of Aruba, learning how to prepare some of the local dishes and those from other neighboring islands. After discovering some fundamental techniques and experimenting with various local products, I was able to define Caribbean cuisine for myself, and began to create some of my own "Caribbean style" dishes. The abundant tropical fruits and chilies that are a cornerstone to Caribbean cooking provide stimulation to all of the senses, from a rainbow of glorious colors to the sweet, sour and hot flavors that jump around on your tongue. And contrary to popular opinion, tropical produce and other ingredients are available in Maine, and elsewhere in the country—you simply need to be flexible.

Caribbean food is influenced by sources almost as numerous as the 7,000 islands that make up the region. The native Indian tribes who originally inhabited the islands relied on pineapple, guavas, black-eyed peas, corn, yams, taro root, peanuts and cassava. The Europeans who arrived in the 15th and 16th centuries created dramatic changes in Caribbean cuisine. The Spaniards introduced onions and garlic while the French, Dutch, Portuguese and English contributed rice, citrus fruit and coffee to the region. The West African slave trade of the early 17th century brought foods like okra, plantains, ackee and breadfruit. Today these foods are staples to many of the islands.

In 1996, I was named Caribbean Chef of the Year after competing against 59 other chefs from 12 countries, in a Caribbean-wide culinary competition. My winning dish, Plantain shrimp with a passion fruit sauce (recipe, page 100), is very representative of Caribbean cuisine. This recipe, along with many others, are among the recipes we prepare in the Caribbean cooking class. Once you understand the differences between plantains and bananas, and you learn the best way to peel and remove the pit from a mango, these products have a better chance of making it into your shopping cart, and you'll be on your way to preparing some of my island recipes, and maybe even creating some of your own.

CARIBBEAN
CUISINE

CARIBBEAN PAPAYA-KAHLUA COLADA

1 CARIBBEAN PAPAYA, ABOUT 3½ POUNDS (OR 3 RIPE
    HAWAIIAN PAPAYAS)
½ CAN (7½ OUNCES) SWEETENED COCONUT CREAM
    (COCO LOPEZ)
2 CUPS PINEAPPLE JUICE
1 CUP KAHLUA (COFFEE-FLAVORED LIQUEUR)
¼ CUP SHREDDED FRESH COCONUT
FRESH PINEAPPLE AND PAPAYA WEDGES FOR GARNISH

1. Peel the papaya and cut in half. Scoop out the seeds and save for the Guava-papaya hot sauce (recipe, page 170) or the Papaya seed dressing (recipe, page 126). Cut the papaya into large chunks and place in a bowl.

2. Place half the papaya in the blender with half of the coconut cream, 1 cup pineapple juice, ½ cup Kahlua and half the shredded coconut. Blend for 1 minute. Add 2 cups crushed or small ice cubes and blend until smooth.

3. Garnish with fresh pineapple and papaya wedges. Once consumed, start again! Do not handle sharp knives at this point.

Mary Jo and I used to stop at the fresh fruit market in Aruba on the way home from work to pick up a few Caribbean papayas for this refreshing island drink. It's a great drink for a hot summer day or to start off a Caribbean-theme party. ■

168 ■ HARTSTONE INN

CARIBBEAN DRY SPICE MIX

4 BAY LEAVES
3 TABLESPOONS DRIED THYME
1 TEASPOON CRUSHED RED PEPPER
1 TEASPOON GROUND CINNAMON
1/2 TEASPOON GROUND NUTMEG
1/2 TEASPOON GROUND ALLSPICE
1/2 TEASPOON GROUND BLACK PEPPER
1/2 TEASPOON GRANULATED GARLIC
1/2 TEASPOON ONION POWDER
1/2 TEASPOON GINGER POWDER
1 TEASPOON GROUND PAPRIKA
1 TEASPOON KOSHER SALT
2 TEASPOONS DRIED BASIL

1. Finely grind the bay leaves in a spice grinder and add the remaining ingredients. Mix well. Store in a jar with a tightly sealed lid.

BATAKONS AND PLANTAIN CHIPS

It is important to use green plantains for these recipes. Ripe-yellow plantains will fall apart. As an hors d'oeuvre, figure one green plantain per person. To peel plantains, score the plantain skin four times lengthwise with a sharp paring knife. Boil water in a large pot and submerge them for 1 minute. Remove from the water and use a paring knife to peel the skin away.

My dry spice mix is a wonderful blend of Caribbean spices and is perfect for grilled meats, seafood and many other uses. A true Jamaican jerk rub is a mixture of onions, scallions, garlic, Scotch Bonnet peppers (habaneros), fresh thyme and various dry spices like allspice, nutmeg, black pepper and cinnamon. Jerk rub is a wet mixture that is rubbed on meats in advance and allowed to marinate. The meats are then smoked or grilled over a wood fire. ■

For Batakons (Colombia) or Tostones (Puerto Rico)

1. Peel the plantains and slice into 1-inch pieces. Keep in a bowl of cold water.

2. In a deep and heavy cast-iron pot or deep-fat fryer, heat 2 inches of vegetable oil to 350 degrees. Remove plantains from the water and pat dry.

3. Deep-fry the plantain pieces for about 5 minutes, until they are browned evenly. Remove and allow them to cool. Press down on the plantains, flattening them to a thickness of $1/2$ inch, and place them back into the cold water. Let them sit in the cold water for 3 minutes, allowing them to swell slightly.

4. Remove them from the water, pat dry and deep-fry once again until they are crispy. Remove, drain on paper towels and season with kosher salt. Serve hot.

For Plantain Chips

1. Peel the plantains and slice lengthwise on the bias into very thin oval strips.

2. Fry the plantains in 350-degree oil until crispy and brown. Drain on paper towels and season with kosher salt.

Guava-Papaya Hot Sauce

4 GUAVAS, PEELED AND ROUGHLY CHOPPED
1 CUP RICE WINE VINEGAR
3 CUPS PAPAYA, PEELED AND SEEDED
2 TABLESPOONS PAPAYA SEEDS
5 HABANERO CHILIES, WITH SEEDS
$1/2$ CUP ROUGHLY CUT RED BELL PEPPER
1 MEDIUM YELLOW ONION, PEELED AND CHOPPED
3 PLUM TOMATOES, CHOPPED
4 CLOVES GARLIC, PEELED AND MINCED

JUICE AND ZEST FROM 1 LIME
1/2 TEASPOON KOSHER SALT
2 TABLESPOONS MUSTARD POWDER

1. Place the guavas and vinegar in a blender and blend until smooth. Strain through a mesh strainer to remove the guava seeds.

2. Discard the seeds and return the strained juice and remaining ingredients to the blender and blend until smooth.

3. Simmer on the stove for 20 minutes, stirring occasionally. Store in covered jars in the refrigerator. *Will keep up to 1 month.*

Mango Hot Sauce

2 MANGOES, PEELED, DESEEDED AND ROUGHLY CHOPPED
5 HABANERO CHILIES, WITH SEEDS
1 RED BELL PEPPER
1 MEDIUM YELLOW ONION, PEELED AND CHOPPED
3 PLUM TOMATOES, CHOPPED
4 CLOVES GARLIC, PEELED AND MINCED
4 TABLESPOONS LIME JUICE
ZEST OF 1 LIME
1 CUP WHITE WINE VINEGAR
1/2 TEASPOON KOSHER SALT
2 TABLESPOONS MUSTARD POWDER

1. Place all items in a blender and blend until smooth.

2. Simmer on the stove for 20 minutes, stirring occasionally. Store in covered jars in the refrigerator. *Will keep up to 1 month.*

Habanero chilies, also known as Scotch Bonnets or Madame Jeanettes, are on the top of the hot scale for chilies. In addition to being hot, habaneros have a wonderful flavor and aroma. Fruit-based hot sauces are very popular in the islands because they blend the heat of the chilies with the sweetness of the fruit. Use these hot sauces on anything from grilled meats and vegetables to seafood. ■

SCABECHI
(ARUBAN PICKLED FISH)

SERVES 6–8

2 POUNDS WHITE FISH FILLETS (COD, HALIBUT, HADDOCK, ETC.), BONELESS AND SKINLESS
2 TABLESPOONS UNSALTED BUTTER
2 SMALL YELLOW ONIONS, SLICED THIN
2 TABLESPOONS CANOLA OIL
1 1/2 CUPS WATER
1/2 CUP WHITE WINE VINEGAR
3 SMALL CARROTS, JULIENNE
1/2 HABANERO CHILI, MINCED WITHOUT SEEDS
2 BAY LEAVES
2 TEASPOONS KOSHER SALT
12 BLACK PEPPERCORNS, WHOLE
2 CLOVES GARLIC, MINCED
1 TABLESPOON CAPERS
8 PIMENTO-STUFFED GREEN OLIVES, SLICED
6 OUNCES BABY SPINACH
PAPAYA SEED DRESSING (RECIPE, PAGE 126)

Scabechi is an Aruban dish of pickled fish. Unlike seviche, which is raw pickled fish, scabechi is made with fish that has been seared and cooked through. Scabechi should be made ahead and refrigerated for at least 24 hours before serving to allow the fish to pick up the flavors from the marinade. This is the perfect dish to prepare ahead of time for a hot summer day picnic. ∎

1. Cut the fish into 4-ounce pieces (about 8 pieces).

2. Heat a large sauté pan over high heat. When hot, add the butter and sauté the fish until golden brown on both sides, about 2 minutes per side, depending on the thickness of the fillets. Place fish in a casserole dish.

3. For the marinade, heat a 2-quart saucepan over medium-high heat and sauté the onions in the oil for 3 minutes. Add the remaining ingredients, up to and

Shrimp come in various sizes and are marketed by these sizes. In the food industry, we refer to shrimp by a number scale, which categorizes shrimp by the number of shrimp to a pound. For example, a 16–20 shrimp, which is extra large in size, would yield between 16 and 20 shrimp per pound. Most markets classify shrimp by size using names like large, small, etc. Following is a guideline used to marry the two schools of thought:

colossal = 10 and under

jumbo = 11–15

extra large = 16–20

large = 21–30

medium = 31–35

small = 36–45

including the garlic, and bring to a boil.

4. Pour the marinade over the fish in the casserole dish and add the capers and olives. Let stand, refrigerated, for at least 24 hours.

5. Remove from the refrigerator 1 hour before serving to warm slightly. Accompany with a small portion of baby spinach tossed with the Papaya seed dressing.

COCONUT–FRIED SHRIMP

SERVES FOUR

20 EXTRA-LARGE RAW SHRIMP (ABOUT 1¼ POUNDS), PEELED AND DEVEINED
KOSHER SALT
2 TABLESPOONS ALL-PURPOSE FLOUR
2 LARGE EGGS, BEATEN, WITH 1 TEASPOON WATER
2 CUPS SHREDDED COCONUT
OPTIONAL: FRESH COCONUT STRIPS
4 CUPS CANOLA OIL FOR FRYING
GUAVA-PAPAYA HOT SAUCE (RECIPE, PAGE 170)

1. Skewer each shrimp lengthwise, tail end last, with a 10-inch bamboo skewer, straightening the shrimp out as it goes on the skewer. Place only one shrimp per skewer, keeping the shrimp at the pointed end of the skewer. Spread the shrimp out on a plate and season with the kosher salt.

2. Dip the shrimp into the flour and coat lightly, shaking off excess flour. Then dip the shrimp into the egg mixture, allowing excess egg to drip off before dipping into the shredded coconut. Turn the shrimp to coat, patting the coconut into the shrimp.

3. Wrap with the fresh coconut strips and secure with a toothpick. Continue with the remaining shrimp.

4. Heat the oil in a deep-fat fryer or a 2-quart saucepan to 350 degrees. Fry the shrimp for 2 minutes, or until golden brown. Serve with Guava-papaya hot sauce.

Keshi Yená

SERVES 4 AS AN APPETIZER

3 TABLESPOONS UNSALTED BUTTER
1 POUND LEAN GROUND BEEF OR CHICKEN
2 RIPE PLUM TOMATOES, CHOPPED
2 MEDIUM YELLOW ONIONS, CHOPPED FINELY
1 SMALL GREEN BELL PEPPER, CHOPPED FINELY
1/2 HABANERO CHILI, MINCED WITHOUT SEEDS
1 TABLESPOON CAPERS
1/4 CUP GREEN OLIVES, CHOPPED
1/4 CUP RAISINS, CHOPPED
1/4 TEASPOON GROUND NUTMEG
KOSHER SALT AND FRESHLY GROUND BLACK PEPPER
1 POUND GOUDA CHEESE, SLICED THINLY
6 OUNCES BABY GREENS
FRUIT SALAD DRESSING OF YOUR CHOICE (RECIPE, PAGE 126)

1. Melt the butter in a large saucepan. Sauté the ground beef, stirring until it is browned. Add the tomatoes, onions, bell peppers and habanero chili. Cook about 5 minutes, until it is almost dry. Remove from the heat and add in the remaining items, except for the cheese, greens and dressing.

The island of Aruba remains part of the Dutch Kingdom, so the Dutch influence is prevalent in everything from architecture to cooking. Keshi Yená is a dish that was originally made by filling an empty shell of a scooped-out Edam cheese with a spiced chicken or beef mixture and baking it. ■

Roti is a flat bread that is very simple and quick to make and resembles a flour tortilla. Roti came to the Caribbean from India and has become a local staple in many islands, especially Trinidad and Tobago. India's influence in Caribbean cuisine is very apparent and curry dishes are a prime example. In Aruba, curried goat stew was very popular and roti is the perfect "utensil" for mopping up the sauce on your plate. Roti can also be filled with ingredients and rolled up to form a sandwich wrap. ∎

2. Butter four 10-ounce ovenproof ramekins. Line with slices of Gouda cheese, overlapping each other. Fill with the beef filling and cover with more slices of Gouda cheese.

3. Boil about 1 quart of water in a teakettle or small saucepot and preheat the oven to 350 degrees.

4. Place the filled ramekins in a roasting pan with high sides and pour boiling water around in the pan. Bake in the preheated oven for about 1 hour.

5. Remove from the oven and let cool slightly. Invert onto a serving dish and serve with a salad of baby greens tossed with your choice of fruit salad dressing.

ROTI BREAD

MAKES 4 FLAT BREADS

2 CUPS ALL-PURPOSE FLOUR
1/4 TEASPOON BAKING POWDER
1/4 TEASPOON SALT
3/4 CUP WATER
1 TEASPOON CANOLA OIL
CANOLA OIL FOR SAUTÉING
KOSHER SALT TO TASTE

1. Mix the flour, baking powder and salt together in a mixing bowl. Make a well with the flour and add the water. Mix in, forming a stiff dough. Knead the dough for 2 minutes and divide into 4 balls.

2. Flatten the balls on a floured work surface with a rolling pin to about half an inch thick. Spread each roti with 1/4 teaspoon canola oil and dust with flour. Form the dough back into a ball by turning the edges into the center, gathering

and pinching the edges, forming the dough into a round shape. Let stand covered with plastic wrap for 30 minutes.

3. Heat a large sauté pan over medium-high heat. On a floured surface, roll out the dough into a flat 8-inch pancake. Cook each side with about $^1/_2$ teaspoon of oil until lightly browned, about 1 to $1^1/_2$ minutes per side. Remove from the pan and sprinkle with kosher salt. Serve hot.

ANNATTO GRILLED SHRIMP WITH A PINEAPPLE-AVOCADO SALSA

SERVES 4

$1^1/_2$ POUNDS EXTRA LARGE RAW SHRIMP, PEELED AND DEVEINED
$^1/_2$ TEASPOON GROUND ANNATTO SEED
3 TABLESPOONS EXTRA VIRGIN OLIVE OIL
2 TABLESPOONS FRESH LIME JUICE
1 TABLESPOON CHOPPED CILANTRO
KOSHER SALT AND BLACK PEPPER TO TASTE
THREE 10-INCH BAMBOO SKEWERS, SOAKED IN WATER
BABY SPINACH, LIME WEDGES AND CILANTRO SPRIGS
    FOR GARNISH

1. Make the Pineapple-avocado salsa (recipe follows).

2. In a small saucepan, heat the olive oil and annatto for a few minutes over a low flame to release the red color. Transfer the olive oil to a small bowl and add the lime juice and chopped cilantro.

3. Thread the shrimp onto the bamboo skewers, sticking each shrimp twice (just above the fin tail, and in the fattest part) and place the skewers on a plate. Brush with the annatto marinade and sprinkle with kosher salt and black pepper.

This is a wonderful dish with its vibrant Caribbean colors and flavors. Annatto, also known as "ruku" in Aruba or achiote seed, is a seed used to color various food products. Since it imparts no flavor into the food, it is popular for coloring foods from butter and margarine to cheese and rice. Annatto is sold as either a whole seed or ground to a fine powder. Frequently it is marketed in the islands as saffron, since it shares the same coloring qualities. Annatto is fat-soluble, so to release its bright color it must be heated in fat or oil. ■

4. Grill the skewers on a hot barbecue or in a hot ribbed grill pan, for 2 minutes on each side (just barely cook through, or they will be dry).

5. Serve over a bed of baby spinach and garnish with mounds of salsa, lime wedges and cilantro sprigs.

PINEAPPLE-AVOCADO SALSA

2 CUPS 1/4-INCH DICE FRESH PINEAPPLE
3 PLUM TOMATOES
2 FIRM-RIPE HAAS AVOCADOS
1 CUP FINELY CHOPPED RED ONION
1/2 CUP CHOPPED FRESH CILANTRO
3 TEASPOONS MINCED FRESH JALAPEÑO CHILE, INCLUDING SEEDS
1/4 CUP FRESH LIME JUICE
1/4 CUP FRESH ORANGE JUICE
1/4 CUP EXTRA-VIRGIN OLIVE OIL
KOSHER SALT AND WHITE PEPPER TO TASTE

1. Core, seed and cut the tomatoes into 1/4-inch dice. Halve, pit and peel the avocado and cut into 1/4-inch dice.

2. Mix together all the ingredients and season with salt and white pepper.

Jerk-Seared Tuna with Mango Salad

SERVES 4

TWO 6-OUNCE TUNA STEAKS, 1 INCH THICK
2 TEASPOONS CANOLA OIL
1 TEASPOON KOSHER SALT
2 TEASPOONS CARIBBEAN DRY SPICE MIX (RECIPE, PAGE 169)
4 SPRIGS CILANTRO AND 4 LIME WEDGES FOR GARNISH

Mango Salad

2 LARGE MANGOES, PITTED, PEELED AND CUT INTO THIN STRIPS
1 MEDIUM RED ONION, JULIENNE
1 RED BELL PEPPER, JULIENNE
1/4 CUP CHOPPED FRESH CILANTRO
1/4 CUP RICE WINE VINEGAR
1 LIME, JUICED
1/4 CUP EXTRA VIRGIN OLIVE OIL
KOSHER SALT AND WHITE PEPPER TO TASTE

1. To make the mango salad, combine all the ingredients and mix well.

2. Sprinkle the tuna steaks with the canola oil and coat thoroughly on both sides. Coat evenly with the salt and Caribbean dry spice mix.

3. Sear the tuna in a hot sauté pan for 3 minutes on each side (should be pink inside). Let stand for 2 minutes and slice thinly on a bias.

4. Divide the fresh mango salad between four plates and fan the sliced tuna on the plates. Garnish with a cilantro sprig and a wedge of lime.

I frequently get sushi-quality tuna from the local seafood market, and tuna that fresh is hard to beat. A simple marinade of Caribbean dry spice and a quick sear in a hot pan yields a tender piece of tuna with a crisp exterior that is rare inside. The mango salad is made with fruit and vegetables cut into thin matchstick-sized strips known as julienne. A julienne cut is a standardized culinary knife cut for food products that measures 1/8 inch by 1/8 inch by 2 inches long. ■

Coconut-Steamed Mussels

SERVES 4

5 POUNDS FRESH MUSSELS, SOAKED, SCRUBBED AND
   BEARDS REMOVED
1/2 CUP DRY WHITE WINE
1 CAN UNSWEETENED COCONUT MILK (14 OUNCES)
3 LIMES, JUICED
2 TABLESPOONS THAI RED CURRY PASTE (RECIPE, PAGE 239)
2 SHALLOTS, MINCED
6 GARLIC CLOVES, MINCED
1 TABLESPOON FISH SAUCE
1 TABLESPOON PALM SUGAR (OR SUBSTITUTE BROWN SUGAR)
1 CUP FRESH CILANTRO SPRIGS (WITH STEMS),
   COARSELY CHOPPED
LIME WEDGES AND CILANTRO SPRIGS FOR GARNISH

1. In a large (9-quart) stockpot, combine the white wine, coconut milk, lime juice, Thai red curry paste, shallots, garlic, fish sauce and palm sugar. Place the pot over high heat and bring to a boil, stirring occasionally.

2. Cook for a few minutes, then add the mussels and mix in. Cover and cook the mussels until opened, about 5 to 8 minutes, stirring occasionally. (Discard any unopened mussels.)

3. Toss the mussels with the cilantro and serve. Garnish with lime wedges and cilantro sprigs.

When I go to purchase fresh mussels, I always look for shells that are closed with a fresh "sea" aroma (not a fishy one). If the shells are open, it means the mussels are not fresh and are beginning to die. Soak the closed mussels in a bowl of cold water for 30 minutes to allow them to purge any sand or grit that may be inside the shell. Gently scrub the shells to remove any debris from the outside and pull on the beard (stringy part protruding from the inside) to remove it and discard. The mussels are now ready to cook. ■

Dim Sum

DIM SUM, which translates to "to touch your heart," is the perfect food for a unique dinner party. Dim sum is a broad term for small individual Chinese delicacies, savory or sweet, ranging from the abundant types of filled dumplings to steamed buns and spring rolls. In the dim sum cooking class, we begin by making numerous dumpling fillings and sauces. We create various dumpling forms or shapes and learn a variety of methods for cooking the dumplings—steaming, deep-fat frying and a combination steaming/pan-frying method used for cooking pot-stickers.

The history of dim sum is directly linked to that of tea consumption. Tea drinking in China can be traced to the Sung dynasty, 960–1280 A.D. As the quality of teas increased over the centuries so did the variety of dim sum. In China's ancient agricultural society, people worked hard all day in the fields and then after work visited a teahouse where they would enjoy fine tea, conversation and a tantalizing selection of dim sum. Today, dim sum are served in many Chinese restaurants with some restaurants specializing in dim sum alone. Dim sum are often served tableside from carts or trays, allowing the patrons to choose from an assortment of various fillings and preparations, enabling everyone to taste a wide variety of these delectable morsels.

At home, a dim sum party is an excellent make-ahead meal. Dim sum, along with the various dipping sauces, can be made earlier that day and kept in the refrigerator until serving time. When your guests arrive, simply set a wok or two on the stove and invite your friends into the kitchen to cook with you.

Forming Dim Sum Dumplings

Following are three recipes for savory dim sum dumpling fillings used for stuffing the many dumpling shapes. Using wonton wrappers (square) and gyoza skins (round), dumplings of various shapes can be formed. The process is a little like filling and forming ravioli. Making dumplings is easy and fun. Take your time forming the various dumplings and don't worry too much about the final shapes—they all end up tasting good. If you are preparing dumplings with multiple fillings, a good trick is to use a different shape for each filling.

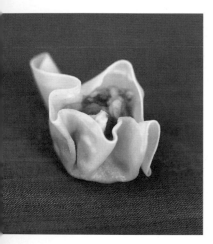

GYOZA SKINS are round. If you can't find the round shape, use a cookie cutter to cut the square wonton wrappers into circles. They can be formed into various shapes by placing 1 teaspoon of filling in the center and wetting the sides. Mentally divide the round circle into 3 wedges, and bring the outside edge of those three wedges to meet in the center, creating a three-sided pyramid dumpling (top photo). Form small pouches, or "shu-mai," (center photo) by gathering up the edges around the filling (leaving the top of the filling exposed) and flattening out the bottom. Half-moons can be formed simply by folding the gyoza skin in half over the filling.

COCKSCOMB DUMPLINGS can be made with a small plastic dumpling press like the one I am using below (also used for empanadas and pierogis), or by hand. Using a gyoza skin, place 1 teaspoon of filling in the center and wet the outside edge. Fold the dumpling in half and press gently all around to seal the dumpling, pressing out any air pockets. Then place the dumpling in the press and gently squeeze, sealing the dumpling and embossing a beautiful "cockscomb" pattern on the curved part of the dumpling. If you don't have a dumpling press, fold small creases into the curved side of the filled, half-moon dumpling. This shape is commonly used for pot-stickers.

WONTON WRAPPERS, on the other hand, are square. These can be formed into triangles by placing 1 teaspoon of the filling in the center, wetting the edges and folding them in half. The square wonton wrappers can also be used to make a pyramid-shape dumpling. Place 1 teaspoon of filling in the center of the wrapper and wet the edges. Bring all 4 corners to the center (over the filling) and press the sides together to form a four-sided pyramid.

Cooking Dim Sum Dumplings

Dumplings can be cooked in various ways. The most common method of cooking is steaming. Bamboo steamers are a very affordable and authentic way to steam dumplings. Bring some water to a boil in a wok, place the dim sum onto lightly oiled bamboo steamer trays and place the covered steamer on the wok. Cook for a few minutes, or until cooked through. It is necessary for the bamboo steamer to be suspended above the water, to allow the steam to rise. If you don't have a wok, you can set the bamboo steamer over a large pan to achieve the same results.

Another popular way to cook dumplings is to deep-fry them in peanut or canola oil until they are crisp and golden. A wok is also the perfect utensil for this cooking method. Place 3 cups oil in the wok and bring to 375 degrees, using a deep-fat thermometer. Gently drop the dumplings into the hot oil in small batches and fry for about 1 minute as the dumpling turns golden brown. Use dumpling shapes where the filling is completely enclosed for deep-frying.

A third method for cooking dumplings is a combination steaming/pan-frying technique used for making pot-stickers. Spread a thin layer of canola oil on the bottom of a large sauté pan and fill the pan with cockscomb dumplings (forming explained on previous page). Pour about 1 cup warm water into the pan (coming about one quarter of the way up the sides of the dumplings) and place the pan over high heat. Cook the dumplings covered for about 2 minutes. Remove the cover and cook until the water completely evaporates. As the water evaporates, the oil is left in the pan and the dumplings begin to brown, sticking to the bottom of the pan, thus the name "pot-sticker." Cook until a nice golden brown crust is formed on the bottom of the dumpling. The top of the dumpling should remain soft from the steaming.

Thai Pork Dumpling Filling

1/2 POUND GROUND PORK

2 CLOVES GARLIC, MINCED

2 TEASPOONS MINCED GINGER

3 TABLESPOONS MINCED RED BELL PEPPER

2 TABLESPOONS CHOPPED CILANTRO

1 TABLESPOON CHOPPED MINT

1/2 CUP MINCED BOK CHOY

3 SCALLIONS, GREEN PART ONLY, FINELY CHOPPED

1/4 TEASPOON SESAME OIL
1 TABLESPOON SOY SAUCE
2 TABLESPOONS SWEET CHILI SAUCE
1 LARGE EGG, BEATEN LIGHTLY

1. In a bowl, combine all of the ingredients and chill for 1 hour.

Turkey and Shiitake Dumpling Filling

1/2 POUND GROUND TURKEY
8 SHIITAKE MUSHROOMS, STEMS REMOVED AND SLICED THIN
4 TABLESPOONS CHOPPED WATER CHESTNUTS
4 SCALLIONS, GREEN PART ONLY, FINELY SLICED
2 TEASPOONS DRY SHERRY
2 TEASPOONS SOY SAUCE
1/2 TEASPOON SESAME OIL
1 TEASPOON GRANULATED SUGAR
PINCH OF KOSHER SALT AND WHITE PEPPER
2 TABLESPOONS CORNSTARCH
1 EGG WHITE, BEATEN

1. In a bowl, combine all of the ingredients and chill for 1 hour.

Shrimp Dumpling Filling

1/2 POUND MEDIUM RAW SHRIMP, PEELED AND DEVEINED
3 SCALLIONS, GREEN PART ONLY, FINELY SLICED
1 TABLESPOON MINCED GINGER

Sweet chili sauce is a bottled sauce available from Asian markets and is made with chilies, vinegar, sugar and garlic. The brand I use is Mae Ploy and it is important to note that there are two types available. The one I prefer is referred to as "sweet chili sauce for chicken" or just plain "sweet chili sauce." The other type is "sweet chili sauce for spring rolls," which has other items added like shredded carrots and turnips that tend to detract from the clean taste of the sauce. ■

3 TABLESPOONS FINELY MINCED CARROT
2 TEASPOONS OYSTER SAUCE
1 TEASPOON SOY SAUCE
1 TEASPOON RICE WINE VINEGAR
1 EGG WHITE, BEATEN

1. Finely chop half the shrimp and place in a bowl.

2. Place the remaining half of the shrimp in a food processor and mince finely.

3. Mix everything together in a bowl and chill for 1 hour.

 Thai Lime Dipping Sauce

2 LIMES, JUICED
1/4 CUP FISH SAUCE
1/4 CUP RICE WINE VINEGAR
1 TABLESPOON GRANULATED SUGAR
1 TABLESPOON MINCED GINGER
1 TABLESPOON SHREDDED FRESH MINT LEAVES
1 TABLESPOON FINELY CHOPPED FRESH CILANTRO

1. Combine all and mix well.

Garlic-Chili Dipping Sauce

1½ TABLESPOONS SAMBAL OELEK (HOT CHILI PASTE)
4 CLOVES GARLIC, MINCED
1/2 CUP RICE WINE VINEGAR

These three dipping sauces represent very different taste and ingredient combinations. The first is a light Thai sauce consisting of lime, fish sauce and vinegar. The second is a spicy garlic and chili dipping sauce packed with a little kick. The third dipping sauce is a more typical soy-based sauce with ginger, garlic and sesame oil. ■

2 TEASPOONS GRANULATED SUGAR
3 SCALLIONS, GREEN PART ONLY, FINELY MINCED
1/2 CUP RICE WINE VINEGAR

1. Combine all and mix well.

Rice vinegar, also referred to as rice wine vinegar, is a Chinese vinegar made from rice wine. Rice vinegar is available in three distinct styles: white, black and red. White rice vinegar is the most common of the rice vinegars and is a clear, mild vinegar with a touch of sweetness. Black rice vinegar, also known as Chinkiang vinegar, is a very dark vinegar with a deep, almost smoky flavor. Red rice vinegar falls in between the white and black rice vinegars in taste and color.

■

Ginger-Sesame Dipping Sauce

1/2 CUP SOY SAUCE
2 CLOVES GARLIC, MINCED
2 TABLESPOONS MINCED FRESH GINGER
2 TABLESPOONS GRANULATED SUGAR
1/2 CUP RICE WINE VINEGAR
1/2 CUP CHINKIANG VINEGAR (IF NOT AVAILABLE, USE RICE WINE VINEGAR)
2 TABLESPOONS SESAME OIL
1/2 TEASPOON EACH BLACK AND REGULAR SESAME SEEDS

1. Combine all and mix well.

Steamed Vegetable Buns

MAKES 24 BUNS

DOUGH

3 TEASPOONS ACTIVE DRY YEAST
1 CUP WARM WATER
1/2 CUP GRANULATED SUGAR
3 CUPS ALL-PURPOSE FLOUR
1 TEASPOON BAKING POWDER

1 TEASPOON SALT

2 TABLESPOONS UNSALTED BUTTER, MELTED

1. Combine the yeast with ¼ cup of the warm water, 2 teaspoons of the sugar and 2 teaspoons of the flour. Mix well, cover and set in a warm place for about 15 minutes, until frothy. (This step assures that the yeast is working.)

2. Mix all ingredients together in a bowl and form a soft dough. Turn out onto a floured surface and knead for 5 minutes. Place the dough into an oiled bowl, cover with plastic wrap and place in a warm place to double in size, about 1 hour.

FILLING

1 TABLESPOON CANOLA OIL

1 CLOVE GARLIC, MINCED

1 TABLESPOON MINCED GINGER

1 CARROT, FINELY SHREDDED

½ CUP MINCED SNOW PEAS, ENDS AND STRINGS REMOVED

1 CUP MINCED BOK CHOY

3 SCALLIONS, GREEN PART ONLY, FINELY SLICED

2 TABLESPOONS SWEET CHILI SAUCE

1 TEASPOON SOY SAUCE

1 TEASPOON SESAME OIL

DIPPING SAUCE OF YOUR CHOICE (RECIPES, PAGES 187–188)

1. Heat the oil in a medium-sized sauté pan. Cook the garlic and ginger for 1 minute in the oil, stirring. Add the carrots, snow peas and bok choy. Cook for 2 minutes, stirring occasionally. Remove to a bowl and add the remaining ingredients. Cool completely.

2. When the dough has doubled in size, remove the cover, punch it down and

As they come out of the bamboo steamer, part of the fun in eating steamed Chinese buns is ripping them open and exposing the luscious filling. "Char Siu Bau" or Chinese barbecue pork buns, are probably the most famous of the steamed buns with a filling made from brightly colored Chinese barbecued pork, ginger, garlic, hoisin sauce, oyster sauce, soy sauce, sesame oil and green onions. ∎

Spring rolls are traditionally served on the first day of the Chinese New Year, which falls in early spring, thus the name "spring rolls." Spring rolls come in many different forms—from Thai fresh spring rolls wrapped in clear rice paper and served uncooked to the Chinese-style spring rolls, which are rolled in a paper-thin pastry wrapper and deep-fried until crispy. ■

turn it out onto a floured surface. Knead again for 5 minutes. Divide the dough into 24 pieces, and roll each piece into a $2^1/_2$-inch circle, keeping them covered under a damp kitchen towel.

3. To fill, put one dough circle in your hand, place 1 Tablespoon of filling in the center of the dough, gather the edges, pinch and twist to seal. Place the buns, sealed side down onto small squares of parchment paper to keep the buns from sticking to the bamboo steamer.

4. Working in batches, place the buns on bamboo steamer trays and steam, covered, over a wok filled with boiling water for 15 minutes. Serve immediately with the dipping sauce.

Crisp Chicken Spring Rolls

MAKES 20 SPRING ROLLS

1 POUND BONELESS AND SKINLESS CHICKEN BREAST,
    CUT INTO THIN STRIPS
1 TABLESPOON CORNSTARCH
1 TEASPOON MUSHROOM SOY SAUCE
2 CLOVES GARLIC, MINCED
2 TABLESPOONS CANOLA OIL
$1/_2$ CUP JULIENNE BAMBOO SHOOTS
$1/_2$ CUP JULIENNE CARROTS
$1/_2$ CUP JULIENNE BOK CHOY
1 PORTABELLA MUSHROOM, JULIENNE
3 TABLESPOONS DRY SHERRY
20 SQUARE SPRING ROLL SKINS
1 LARGE EGG, BEATEN FOR SEALING
CANOLA OIL FOR DEEP-FRYING
THAI LIME DIPPING SAUCE (RECIPE, PAGE 187)

1. Combine the chicken with the cornstarch, mushroom soy sauce and garlic. Heat the 2 Tablespoons of oil in a sauté pan over medium-high heat and cook the chicken mixture for 2 minutes, stirring. Add the bamboo shoots, carrots, bok choy and portabella mushroom and continue cooking for 1 minute more. Add the sherry and reduce for 1 minute. Turn the mixture into a colander to let the filling cool and drain, discarding the liquid.

2. To roll the spring rolls, place the spring roll skins on the counter and cover with a damp kitchen towel. Lay one skin out with a corner facing you. Brush the top and 2 side corners with the beaten egg. Spoon 2 Tablespoons of filling about 2 inches from the bottom corner, and form into a band, horizontally. Fold the bottom corner over the filling and roll halfway, completely enclosing the filling. Fold in the side corners, pressing down to seal and finish rolling the spring roll. Place on a sheet covered with parchment paper and keep covered with a moist kitchen towel while you continue rolling the remaining spring rolls.

3. To cook, heat the oil for deep-frying to 375 degrees in either a deep-fat fryer, wok or saucepan. Fry only 5 spring rolls at a time (do not overcrowd). Turn and fry until crisp and golden brown, about 2 minutes. Remove the crisp spring rolls with a slotted spoon and drain on paper towels. Repeat with the remaining spring rolls and serve immediately with the Thai lime dipping sauce.

$\mathcal{L}$OBSTER TOAST

SERVES 4

TWO 1¼ POUND LIVE MAINE LOBSTERS OR 1 POUND
    RAW, PEELED AND DEVEINED SHRIMP
2 TEASPOONS CORNSTARCH (IF USING LOBSTER)
2 TEASPOONS MINCED GINGER

For this recipe I took a traditional Asian dish, shrimp toast, and used Maine lobster to create a recipe with a Maine twist. The shrimp version (also explained in the recipe) is much easier and quicker to produce since the meat is easily removed from its shell, or can easily be purchased pre-peeled. Raw lobster meat sticks to the shell, so in this recipe I blanch the lobster quickly—just enough to release the meat from the shell.

5 SCALLIONS, GREEN PART ONLY, CHOPPED

2 TABLESPOONS SOY SAUCE

1 TEASPOON SESAME OIL

1 EGG WHITE

4 LARGE EGGS

1 CUP CANOLA OIL

4 SLICES WHITE SANDWICH BREAD

GINGER-SESAME DIPPING SAUCE (RECIPE, PAGE 188)

1. For lobster toast, boil 2 quarts of water in a 4-quart saucepan. Immerse the lobsters head first into the boiling water and cook for 3 minutes. Immediately remove the lobsters from the water and cool. This will only partially cook the lobsters. When the lobsters are cool enough to handle, remove the meat from the knuckles, claws and tail (discarding the vein). Pat the lobster meat dry with paper towels and cut into 1-inch pieces. Toss the lobster meat in cornstarch.

2. In a food processor, mince the lobster or shrimp. Add the ginger, scallions, soy sauce, sesame oil and the egg white. Process again to combine.

3. Lay out the bread slices and cut off the crust. Divide and spread the lobster or shrimp mixture onto the bread slices. Cut each bread slice in quarters from corner to corner, creating 4 small triangles.

4. Whisk the eggs together in a bowl.

5. Heat a large skillet and add the vegetable oil. Dip the bread triangles into the egg wash and fry in the hot oil, meat side down first, then turn over and cook on the other side until golden brown. Drain on paper towels. Serve warm with the Ginger-sesame dipping sauce.

H

Hors d'Oeuvres

I ORIGINALLY created this cooking class to instruct students on a make-ahead holiday cocktail party. Hors d'oeuvres, however, are much more than just holiday fare. If you intend to throw a party and would like to do more mingling with your guests than with your food, I suggest that you throw an hors d'oeuvre party and offer a variety of them.

Hors d'oeuvres are typically finger foods that can be consumed while standing, which means you don't have to have individual seating arrangements for each guest. The recipes I have included in this section range from spicy nuts offered in bowls to Onion, sage and olive tartlets, and Pear and Gorgonzola toasts, which can be arranged beautifully on trays or platters. Throughout the cooking class section of this book, there are many more recipes that are also well-suited for such an occasion.

There are a few things to keep in mind when planning a menu for a cocktail party. Offer a variety of foods from meats and seafood options to vegetable and cheese selections. Choose recipes that utilize various cooking methods so you don't end up with a table full of fried foods, for example. Create a balance of cold foods that can be prepared and ready before the party begins, and hot items that can be prepared ahead of time, but need to be cooked or heated at the last minute.

HORS D'OEUVRES

PEAR AND GORGONZOLA TOASTS

SERVES 6–8

1 LOAF MULTIGRAIN SLICED SANDWICH BREAD
EXTRA VIRGIN OLIVE OIL, AS NEEDED
10 OUNCES GORGONZOLA CHEESE
5 TABLESPOONS HEAVY CREAM
2 BARTLETT OR RED PEARS
1/4 CUP PECAN HALVES, SLICED THINLY

1. Remove the crust from the bread. Cut each slice in half crosswise, making "fingers" that are about $1^1/2$ inches by 3 inches.

2. Brush a large sauté pan lightly with olive oil and place over medium heat. In batches, toast the bread in the pan, oiling the pan as necessary.

3. Using a fork, mix the Gorgonzola with the heavy cream to achieve a soft, spreadable, but not too runny, consistency.

4. Spread a heaping teaspoon of the cheese on each bread finger.

5. Cut the pears in half and use a melon baller to scoop out the core. Thinly slice the pear into wedges. Top the cheese with a pear slice and garnish with the sliced pecans.

White Bean and Avocado Salsa

SERVES 4–6

2 FIRM-RIPE HAAS AVOCADOS
2 VINE-RIPENED TOMATOES
$1/2$ MEDIUM RED ONION
1 CUP COOKED SMALL WHITE BEANS
1 LIME, JUICED
2 TABLESPOONS EXTRA VIRGIN OLIVE OIL
$1/4$ CUP CHOPPED FRESH CILANTRO
KOSHER SALT AND FRESHLY GROUND BLACK PEPPER TO TASTE

1. Halve, pit, and peel the avocado.

2. Cut the tomato and red onion into a small dice and dice the avocado into $1/2$-inch cubes.

Throughout this cookbook I refer to terms that describe some of the basic knife cuts, which are standard in kitchens everywhere. So here is some further clarification. A julienne cut is a long rectangular shape that measures $1/8$ inch by $1/8$ inch by 2 inches long. Diced vegetables have four ranges:

brunoise ($1/8$-inch square)

small dice ($1/4$-inch square)

medium dice ($1/3$-inch square)

large dice ($3/4$-inch square)

3. Fold all ingredients together and season to taste. Set aside for 1–2 hours to let the flavors develop.

4. Serve with Spiced pita crisps (recipe follows).

Spiced Pita Crisps

MAKES 96 CRISPS

1 TEASPOON KOSHER SALT
1 TEASPOON GROUND CAYENNE PEPPER
1/2 TEASPOON CHILI POWDER
1/2 TEASPOON GROUND CUMIN
1/4 TEASPOON GROUND ALLSPICE
SIX 6-INCH PITAS
ABOUT 1/4 CUP EXTRA VIRGIN OLIVE OIL
1/2 CUP FINELY SHREDDED PARMESAN CHEESE

1. Preheat the oven to 375 degrees.

2. Combine the salt and ground spices.

3. Split each pita horizontally into 2 rounds and brush rough sides with the oil. Cut each round into 8 wedges and arrange with oiled sides up on baking sheets. Sprinkle the pita wedges with the spices and Parmesan.

4. Bake 12 to 15 minutes, or until golden. *Crisps may be made up to 3 days ahead and kept in an airtight container at room temperature.*

Pita crisps are simple to prepare and are the perfect accompaniment to hummus (a Middle Eastern dip made from chickpeas), tapenade or any other dip for that matter. When I worked on Block Island, we served pita crisps with hummus and what we called "antipasto salad," which consisted of equal parts of 1/2-inch chopped roasted peppers, marinated artichoke hearts, ripe olives, green olives, celery and red onion. ■

BLACK PEPPER ALMONDS

Last year I made these spicy almonds just before the holidays, packaged them up in cellophane bags and gave them away as Christmas presents. They were very well received and are truly addicting. The brown sugar gives a hint of sweetness, just enough to offset the heat from the black pepper. Whole nuts of any kind can be substituted for the almonds. You can use one type of nut or a selection of various whole nuts. ■

1 TABLESPOON TABLE-GRIND BLACK PEPPER
2 TEASPOONS KOSHER SALT
$1/4$ CUP, PLUS 1 TEASPOON UNSALTED BUTTER
$3/4$ CUP BROWN SUGAR, FIRMLY PACKED
4 TEASPOONS WATER
$2^{1}/_{2}$ CUPS WHOLE ALMONDS

1. Preheat the oven to 350 degrees.

2. Line a baking sheet with foil and lightly butter the foil with the 1 teaspoon of butter. Mix the black pepper and salt together in a small bowl.

3. Melt the remaining $1/4$ cup butter in a large nonstick skillet over medium-low heat. Add the sugar and 4 teaspoons water; stir until sugar dissolves. Add the almonds; toss to coat. Cook over medium heat until syrup thickens and the almonds are well coated, stirring occasionally, about 5 minutes. Sprinkle half of the pepper mixture over the almonds.

4. Transfer the almonds to the lined baking sheet, using a metal spatula to quickly separate the almonds. Sprinkle the remaining pepper mixture over the nuts. Bake until deep golden brown, about 10 minutes. Transfer the baking sheet to a rack and cool. *Store in an airtight container at room temperature for up to 1 week.*

CRISP SPICED NUTS

2 EGG WHITES
1 1/2 TEASPOONS KOSHER SALT
3/4 CUP GRANULATED SUGAR
2 TEASPOONS WORCESTERSHIRE SAUCE
2 TABLESPOONS GROUND SWEET PAPRIKA
1 1/2 TEASPOONS GROUND CAYENNE PEPPER
1 1/2 CUPS WHOLE ALMONDS (ABOUT 1/2 POUND)
1 1/2 CUPS WHOLE HAZELNUTS (ABOUT 1/2 POUND)
1 1/2 CUPS WHOLE PECANS (ABOUT 1/2 POUND)
6 TABLESPOONS UNSALTED BUTTER, MELTED AND COOLED

1. Preheat the oven to 325 degrees.

2. Beat the egg whites in a mixer until they are very foamy. Gradually beat in the salt, sugar, Worcestershire sauce, paprika and cayenne. Stir in the nuts and melted butter, combining well, and spread out onto a baking sheet.

3. Bake nuts in the middle of the oven, stirring every 10 minutes, until crisp and golden, about 30 to 40 minutes. Spread the nuts on a sheet of foil and cool. Break up any nut clusters. *Nuts may be made 1 week ahead and kept in an airtight container at room temperature.*

DRIED APRICOTS WITH BOURSIN AND PISTACHIOS

Dried apricots offer a wonderful alternative to the standard toast-based hors d'oeuvre. I use the herbed Boursin cheese in this recipe, but the pepper-flavored Boursin can also be used if you like the extra heat. In addition, the cheese mixture is good on celery sticks, toast rounds, apple slices or hollowed-out cherry tomatoes. ■

SERVES 6

1 POUND DRIED APRICOT HALVES
3/4 CUP FRESH ORANGE JUICE
3 TABLESPOONS GRAND MARNIER (ORANGE LIQUEUR)
1/4 CUP SHELLED PISTACHIOS, TOASTED
KOSHER SALT
4 OUNCES CREAM CHEESE
1 PACKAGE HERBED BOURSIN CHEESE, CHILLED

1. Place the apricots in a medium-sized bowl with the orange juice and Grand Marnier. Let stand, tossing occasionally, for 20 minutes.

2. Chop the pistachios coarsely by hand and season with kosher salt.

3. Drain the apricots on paper towels. Place the apricot halves on a baking sheet, cut side up.

4. In a mixer, blend the cream cheese until smooth. Add the Boursin and mix to combine.

5. Using a piping bag fitted with a small star tip, pipe stars of the Boursin mixture around the top of each apricot and sprinkle with the chopped pistachios. These may be made 1 day in advance. Keep single layered in an airtight container.

Onion, Sage and Olive Tartlets

MAKES 20 TARTLETS

1 BATCH PASTRY DOUGH (RECIPE, PAGE 67)
1 POUND YELLOW ONIONS (3 MEDIUM-SIZED ONIONS), SLICED
2 SLICES THICK BACON, FINELY DICED
1 TEASPOON GRANULATED SUGAR
1/2 TEASPOON KOSHER SALT
2 TO 3 TEASPOONS BALSAMIC VINEGAR
2 TABLESPOONS FINELY CHOPPED FRESH SAGE
1/2 CUP KALAMATA OLIVES, PITTED AND COARSELY CHOPPED
FRESHLY GROUND BLACK PEPPER
1/4 CUP HEAVY CREAM
1 LARGE EGG
1/4 CUP FRESHLY GRATED PARMESAN CHEESE

1. Lay small 2-inch tartlet molds out on a baking sheet and lightly coat with vegetable cooking spray. Remove the dough from the refrigerator and roll it out on the counter, to $1/8$-inch thickness, using flour as necessary to prevent it from sticking. Dust off excess flour and cut into 3-inch circles. Lay a dough circle over a tartlet mold and press into the mold. Trim excess dough. Continue with the remaining shells.

2. Preheat the oven to 350 degrees. Cover the shells with a small round of parchment paper (just to cover), and fill the paper and shells with pie weights or raw beans to prevent the tartlet shells from swelling. Bake for 10 minutes, remove from the oven and empty out the pie weights/beans and parchment paper. Return the tartlet shells to the oven to bake for 10 more minutes.

3. Peel the onions and cut them in half from root to tip. Cut out the dense core

These tartlets are unique and quite tasty. When onions are caramelized, they become very sweet and are the perfect accompaniment to the salty olives, fresh sage and Parmesan cheese. I have some barquette molds, which are boat-shaped tartlet pans that measure about 3 inches long, and they work perfectly for these tartlets. ■

at the root end and slice the onions $1/4$-inch thick, again from root end to tip. In a large (4-quart) saucepan over medium-high heat, cook the bacon until almost crisp, stirring often. Add the onions, sugar, and salt, and cook, stirring often until they cook down by two-thirds, about 10 minutes. Add 2 teaspoons vinegar, reduce the heat to medium, and continue to cook until the onions are an even golden brown and softened to a marmalade consistency, 15 to 20 minutes, depending on the onions. Stir often and scrape up any brown bits clinging to the bottom of the pan. Near the end, the onions need to be stirred constantly to prevent them from sticking and burning.

4. Stir in the sage and kalamata olives and allow the mixture to cool slightly. Taste and adjust seasoning with black pepper and kosher salt if needed.

5. Preheat the oven to 350 degrees if not still on from step 2.

6. Stir the cream, egg and Parmesan into the caramelized onions until thoroughly combined. Divide the filling among the tartlet shells and spread evenly with the back of a spoon.

7. Bake in the upper third of the oven until the filling is set, about 15 minutes. The filling should still be soft but not runny. Let cool slightly and serve.

Tomato Salsa with Homemade Corn Tortilla Chips

1 MEDIUM RED ONION
1 MEDIUM GREEN BELL PEPPER
3 CLOVES GARLIC
3 HABANERO CHILIES, WITHOUT SEEDS
10 PLUM TOMATOES
3 LIMES, JUICED

I developed this Tomato Salsa recipe for my friend Kim who used to frequently ask me to make it for her in Aruba. When she moved off island, I wrote the recipe down for her and she continues to make it on a regular basis. If you can't find habanero chilies at your market, jalapeños are a suitable substitute. The three habaneros will produce a very hot salsa, so I suggest that you add a little at a time until you reach the desired level of heat.

1 BUNCH CILANTRO (½ CUP CHOPPED)
4 CUPS TOMATO JUICE
KOSHER SALT

1. Roughly chop the onion and green bell pepper.

2. Mince the garlic and the habanero (discarding the lethal seeds).

3. Place all four in the bowl of a food processor and process lightly for 5 seconds.

4. Remove the core from the tomatoes, and cut in half width-wise. Squeeze out the seeds (discarding them) and roughly cut the tomatoes. Add to the food processor, and blend for 10 seconds.

5. Add the lime juice and chopped cilantro to the bowl and blend for 5 seconds. Add half the tomato juice to the food processor and blend for another 5 seconds. Remove to a kitchen bowl and stir in the remaining tomato juice. Season with salt to taste. Adjust heat by the amount and type of hot chilies used.

HOMEMADE CORN TORTILLA CHIPS

24 SIX-INCH CORN TORTILLAS
1 QUART CANOLA OIL FOR FRYING
KOSHER SALT TO TASTE

1. Cut the tortillas into 6 wedges.

2. In a large 9-quart stockpot, bring the oil to 375 degrees on a deep-fat thermometer.

3. Fry the wedges, 8 at a time, until crisp, about 1 minute. Using a slotted spoon, remove the chips to a pan lined with paper towels to drain. Sprinkle the chips with kosher salt to taste. Continue with the remaining chips. *Chips will keep in an airtight container for 2 days.*

My tomato salsa recipe makes a salsa that is quite smooth. If you prefer a chunkier salsa, dice the red onion, green bell pepper and tomatoes into ½-inch cubes. Add the minced garlic and chilies, the lime juice and cilantro. Reduce the amount of tomato juice by one half, mix everything together and season with salt. Salsa is at its best after it has had a few hours to rest, which allows the flavors to develop and combine. ■

POTATO AND APPLE PANCAKES WITH SMOKED SALMON

Potato pancakes are quite adaptable on menus. For breakfast I serve them nestled under a baked egg or as a starter smothered with sautéed apples and pears. At dinner I serve an appetizer in which I substitute half of the red potato with shredded sweet potato and serve the cakes with sautéed shrimp in a vermouth beurre blanc. ■

SERVES 6

1 POUND RED POTATOES, PEELED
1 MEDIUM YELLOW ONION, PEELED
1 MEDIUM GRANNY SMITH APPLE, UNPEELED,
   QUARTERED AND CORED
2 LARGE EGGS
2 SCALLIONS, GREEN PART ONLY, FINELY CHOPPED
3/4 TEASPOON KOSHER SALT
1/2 TEASPOON GROUND BLACK PEPPER
1/2 CUP ALL-PURPOSE FLOUR
CANOLA OIL (FOR FRYING)
4 OUNCES SOUR CREAM
2 TABLESPOONS CHOPPED RED ONION
4 OUNCES THINLY SLICED SMOKED SALMON
1 TABLESPOON CHOPPED FRESH CHIVES

1. Using a food processor fitted with a coarse shredding disc, grate the potatoes, onion and apple at the same time. Transfer the mixture to a colander set in the sink and lined with a lint-free kitchen towel. Gather the towel tightly around the potato mixture and squeeze out as much liquid as possible.

2. Place the potato mixture, eggs, scallions, salt and black pepper in a bowl; toss to blend. Mix in the flour.

3. Preheat the oven to 300 degrees.

4. Heat a large sauté pan over medium-high heat. Pour enough canola oil into the pan to cover the bottom. Working in batches, drop heaping Tablespoons of

the potato mixture into the skillet for each pancake. Flatten each mound with the spoon to form a 2-inch round cake. Fry until cooked through and crisp, about 2 minutes per side. Transfer the potato cakes to a baking sheet and keep warm in the preheated oven while you continue with the remaining potato mixture.

5. Garnish the pancakes with the smoked salmon and a dollop of the sour cream. Sprinkle with red onion and chives and serve.

Smoked Salmon — With my own smoker on property, I am able to smoke all kinds of seafood, cured with various spice mixes and smoked with various woods. I smoke all of my seafood with fruitwoods like cherry and apple, while meats and sausages I smoke with hickory and mesquite. The fatty flesh of salmon makes it a prime candidate for smoking and its versatility allows me to incorporate it in menus from breakfast to dinner. ■

PASTA DISHES play a key role in the diets of many people, yet few of us actually prepare pasta from scratch. Dry pasta is very convenient and fresh pastas are now readily available at major supermarkets. Fresh pasta, however, is simple to make, and there is something utterly satisfying about eating pasta made by your own hands. In my Pasta Pasta Pasta cooking class, we begin by creating various flavored pasta doughs. Participants learn how to roll out the dough to create a wide variety of shapes from farfalle to fettuccine, and how to create filled pastas like ravioli and tortellini. I demonstrate the best way to cook fresh pasta and we finish the pasta dishes with various sauces and meats.

The origin of pasta is a very controversial subject in culinary history. The Arabic countries, Italy and China have all laid claim to the creation of what has become a favorite food worldwide. Most probably, different versions of pasta were made in various parts of the world as a way to preserve grains. Early pasta makers would grind the grains, mix them with water and dry the mixture, which had the added advantage of cooking quickly. It was the Italians, however, who perfected pasta. The earliest evidence of its existence was found in Etruscan tombs that date back to 4 B.C., where a wall picture contains instruments used in making pasta, including a pastry board, a rolling pin and a pastry cutter.

Variations of these tools are still used in making pasta today, along with a few technical advances. I got my first pasta machine when I was 20 years old and have been using it ever since. The brand I have is an "Atlas" machine and the references I make to the thickness of the pasta will relate to the numbers on the dial of this machine. Most kitchen stores stock these hand-powered machines and it is a wise investment if you like pasta. My machine has two attachments: a fettuccine/spaghetti cutter and a ravioli maker. I recommend these two attachments, and there are numerous other ones available. If you don't have a pasta machine, rolling the pasta by hand is a little more work, but can be done. Fresh pasta cooks much faster than dried pasta, so pay close attention to it while it is cooking.

Pasta
Pasta
Pasta

ASTA DOUGH

EGG PASTA DOUGH (PLAIN)

2½ CUPS PASTA FLOUR (SEMOLINA)
2 LARGE EGGS, LIGHTLY BEATEN
1 TEASPOON SALT
1 TABLESPOON EXTRA VIRGIN OLIVE OIL
¼ CUP WARM WATER

1. Place the flour on a clean working counter and make a well in the center. Add the remaining ingredients to the center of the well and gradually mix the dry ingredients into the wet, forming a smooth-soft dough (adding additional water if necessary to make the dough soft).

2. Knead the dough 10 minutes, wrap tightly with plastic wrap and refrigerate for 1 hour.

3. This recipe makes a little over 1 pound of dough.

SPINACH PASTA DOUGH

3½ CUPS PASTA FLOUR (SEMOLINA)
5 OUNCES FRESH SPINACH, COARSELY CHOPPED
2 TABLESPOONS PLUS WARM WATER
1 LARGE EGG, LIGHTLY BEATEN
1 TEASPOON SALT
1 TABLESPOON EXTRA VIRGIN OLIVE OIL

1. In a blender, puree the spinach, water and egg until smooth.

2. Place the flour on a clean working counter and make a well in the center. Add the spinach liquid, salt and olive oil to the center of the well and gradually

mix the dry ingredients into the wet, forming a smooth-soft dough (adding additional water if necessary to make the dough soft).

3. Knead the dough 10 minutes, wrap tightly with plastic wrap and refrigerate for 1 hour.

4. This recipe makes a little over 1¹/₂ pounds of dough.

BEET PASTA DOUGH

2¹/₂ CUPS PASTA FLOUR (SEMOLINA)
1 LARGE EGG, LIGHTLY BEATEN
2 TEASPOONS PLUS WARM WATER
¹/₂ POUND COOKED FRESH OR CANNED BEETS,
    COARSELY CHOPPED
1 TEASPOON SALT
1 TABLESPOON EXTRA VIRGIN OLIVE OIL

1. In a blender, puree the beets, egg and water until smooth.

2. Place the flour on a clean working counter and make a well in the center. Add the beet liquid, salt and olive oil to the center of the well and gradually mix the dry ingredients into the wet, forming a smooth-soft dough (adding additional water if necessary to make the dough soft).

3. Knead the dough 10 minutes, wrap tightly with plastic wrap and refrigerate for 1 hour.

4. This recipe makes a little over 1 pound of dough.

SHAPING THE PASTA

1. Once your pasta has set up for at least 1 hour in the refrigerator, remove it from the plastic and press it down into a disk on a floured (semolina) work surface. Cut the dough into 4 equal pieces and rewrap 3 of the pieces in the

Cooked fresh beets will yield a dough with the brightest red color, so I always recommend using fresh beets over canned. To cook the beets, remove the greens from the top of the beets, wash them and place them in a saucepan with their skins on. Cover the beets with cold water, bring to a boil and reduce to a simmer. Cook until the beets are fork tender. Smaller beets will cook quicker. Plunge the beets into cold water for a few minutes to cool, and then work off the skins with your hands. Roughly cut the beets into large chunks. ∎

plastic wrap to prevent them from drying out.

2. With a rolling pin and extra semolina (if needed), roll the dough out to about $^1/_4$ inch thick. If the dough seems sticky, dust it with some semolina.

3. Set up the pasta machine with a setting of 1 (the highest, thickest setting) and roll the pasta through. Again, if the dough seems sticky, dust it with some semolina. Adjust the thickness to either setting 5 or 6, depending on the pasta shape you are making, and run the dough through the machine at that setting.

4. Lay the dough out on a floured work surface and follow the guidelines below to make various shapes (scraps can be reworked into a ball and used again). For longer storage of the pasta, dry it overnight (make sure it is well coated with semolina to prevent it from sticking) at room temperature. *Store the pasta in freezer bags. Pasta freezes well, and can be kept for up to 3 months.*

FETTUCCINE OR SPAGHETTI BY MACHINE: Roll out to setting 6, and cut the sheet into 10-inch sections. Feed the sheet through the fettuccine or spaghetti attachment on the machine. Dry in a single layer on a baking sheet dusted with semolina.

FETTUCCINE OR LINGUINE BY HAND: With a rolling pin, roll out the dough until it is $^1/_{16}$-inch thin. Cut the sheet into 10-inch sections. Dust the sections with semolina and roll them up. Using a knife, cut the roll of pasta into strips (fettuccine $^1/_4$ inch and linguine $^1/_8$ inch). Unroll the strips and dry in a single layer on a baking sheet dusted with semolina.

FARFALLE: Roll out to setting 6, and use a serrated pastry wheel to cut the pasta in $1^1/_4$-inch strips. Cut the strips into $2^1/_2$-inch long rectangular sections. To form, place your index finger on the exact center of the rectangular piece of dough and with your other hand, pinch on the narrow sides toward the index finger, forming a bow tie shape. Dry in a single layer on a baking sheet dusted with semolina.

PAPPARDELLE: Roll out to setting 5, and cut the sheet into 10-inch sections. Dust the sections with semolina and roll them up. Using a knife, cut the roll of pasta into strips 1 inch wide. Unroll the strips and dry in a single layer on a baking sheet dusted with semolina.

Spinach Fettuccine Puttanesca with Shrimp

SERVES 4

1 TABLESPOON SALT
2 TABLESPOONS EXTRA VIRGIN OLIVE OIL
1 POUND EXTRA-LARGE RAW SHRIMP, PEELED AND DEVEINED
1 BATCH SPINACH PASTA DOUGH, CUT AS FETTUCCINE
    (RECIPE, PAGE 208)
1 SHALLOT, MINCED
1/4 CUP CHOPPED SUN-DRIED TOMATOES
1/4 CUP COUNTRY MIXED OLIVES, PITTED
1 CUP MARINARA SAUCE (HOMEMADE OR YOUR FAVORITE BRAND)
KOSHER SALT AND FRESHLY GROUND BLACK PEPPER TO TASTE

1. Fill a large pot 3/4 full of water and bring to a boil with 1 Tablespoon salt.

2. Heat a large sauté pan over medium heat and add the olive oil. Add the shrimp and cook on one side for 1 minute.

3. Drop the spinach fettuccine in the boiling water and cook for 7 minutes or until al dente, stirring occasionally.

4. Turn the shrimp over and add the minced shallot. Cook for another minute.

Add the sun-dried tomatoes and olives and toss. Pour in the marinara sauce and stir, heating the sauce through.

5. Strain the pasta, allowing all of the water to drain off, and add it to the pan with the sauce. Mix the pasta in with the sauce and adjust the seasoning with salt and pepper. Serve immediately.

Spaghetti with a Creamy Prosciutto and Roasted Pepper Sauce

SERVES 4

1 TABLESPOON SALT
2 TABLESPOONS EXTRA VIRGIN OLIVE OIL
1 SHALLOT, MINCED
1/4 CUP DRY WHITE WINE
1 BATCH EGG PASTA DOUGH, CUT AS SPAGHETTI
   (RECIPE, PAGE 208)
2/3 CUP HEAVY CREAM
1/4 POUND THINLY SLICED PROSCIUTTO, COARSELY CHOPPED
1/2 CUP MEDIUM DICE ROASTED RED PEPPERS
KOSHER SALT AND FRESHLY GROUND BLACK PEPPER TO TASTE
1/4 CUP FRESHLY GRATED ASIAGO CHEESE

1. Fill a large pot 3/4 full of water and bring to a boil with 1 Tablespoon salt.

2. Heat a large sauté pan over medium heat and add the olive oil. Add the minced shallot and stir for 1 minute, cooking the shallot. Deglaze with white wine and reduce until dry.

3. Drop the spaghetti in the boiling water and cook for 5 minutes or until al dente, stirring occasionally.

Prosciutto is the Italian word for ham. Unlike American ham, prosciutto is not smoked, it is simply seasoned, cured and air-dried. In Italy, each prosciutto is named after the town in which it is made. For example, prosciutto di Parma comes from the town of Parma in northern Italy. Prosciutto is now widely produced here in the United States as well. Prosciutto is best when it is sliced extremely thin and served in its raw form. ■

4. Add the heavy cream to the sauté pan, and reduce for 1 minute. Add the prosciutto and roasted red pepper to the sauce and stir, heating it through.

5. Strain the pasta, allowing all of the water to drain off, and add it to the pan with the sauce. Mix the pasta in with the sauce and adjust the seasoning with salt and pepper. Serve immediately topped with the freshly grated Asiago cheese.

PAPPARDELLE WITH PESTO AND OVEN-ROASTED TOMATOES

SERVES 4

8 PLUM TOMATOES
2 TABLESPOONS EXTRA VIRGIN OLIVE OIL
KOSHER SALT AND FRESHLY GROUND BLACK PEPPER TO TASTE
1 TABLESPOON SALT
1 BATCH EGG PASTA DOUGH, CUT AS PAPPARDELLE
    (RECIPE, PAGE 208)
1/4 CUP EXTRA VIRGIN OLIVE OIL
1 SHALLOT, MINCED
1 BATCH PESTO (RECIPE, PAGE 220)
1/4 CUP FRESHLY GRATED PARMESAN CHEESE

1. Preheat the oven to 375 degrees. Line a baking sheet with parchment paper and brush the paper with 1 teaspoon of the olive oil.

2. Cut the plum tomatoes in half lengthwise and place them cut side up on the baking sheet. Drizzle the tomatoes with the remainder of the 2 Tablespoons of olive oil and sprinkle the tomatoes with kosher salt and freshly ground black pepper. Bake in the preheated oven for 2 hours.

3. Fill a large pot 3/4 full of water and bring to a boil with 1 Tablespoon salt.

Pappardelle is a wide noodle that creates a very rustic-looking pasta dish. The sheer volume of pasta in each forkful makes pappardelle my favorite pasta to eat. Pesto is a perfect match for flat pasta because it will stick to anything, while a nice thin cream sauce would simply run right off. When tomatoes are oven-roasted, the flavors become concentrated and nicely intense. ■

4. Heat a large sauté pan over medium heat and add the $^1/_4$ cup olive oil. Add the minced shallot and stir for 1 minute, cooking the shallot.

5. Drop the pappardelle in the boiling water and cook for 9 minutes or until al dente, stirring occasionally.

6. Reduce the heat of the sauté pan to low, add the Pesto and stir.

7. Strain the pasta, allowing all of the water to drain off, and add it to the pan with the sauce. Mix the pasta in with the sauce and adjust the seasoning with salt and pepper. Serve immediately topped with the freshly grated Parmesan and the oven-roasted tomatoes.

Farfalle with fresh Tomato, Basil and Roasted Garlic

SERVES 4

1 HEAD GARLIC
1 TEASPOON EXTRA VIRGIN OLIVE OIL
1 TABLESPOON SALT
3 MEDIUM VINE-RIPE TOMATOES
2 TABLESPOONS EXTRA VIRGIN OLIVE OIL
1 SHALLOT, MINCED
1 BATCH EGG PASTA DOUGH, CUT AS FARFALLE
   (RECIPE, PAGE 208)
$^1/_4$ CUP CHOPPED FRESH BASIL
KOSHER SALT AND FRESHLY GROUND BLACK PEPPER TO TASTE
$^1/_4$ CUP FRESHLY GRATED PARMESAN CHEESE

1. Preheat the oven to 400 degrees. Cut the very top off the whole head of garlic, just exposing the tops of the cloves, and drizzle with 1 teaspoon olive oil. Place the garlic on an ovenproof plate or pan and roast in the oven for 1 hour.

Farfalle is a bow tie-shaped pasta that can be made to any desired size. Once you have learned the technique for forming farfalle, they can be made quite quickly. The quaint shape of farfalle makes them a perfect candidate for pasta salads. ■

Remove from the oven and cool for 5 minutes. Squeeze the head of garlic from the bottom up, forcing the soft cloves to ooze out of the top openings. Discard the shell and reserve the roasted garlic.

2. Fill a large pot ³/₄ full of water and bring to a boil with 1 Tablespoon salt.

3. Remove the cores from the tomatoes and cut them in half around their equators. Gently squeeze out the tomato seeds and dice the tomatoes into ¹/₂-inch pieces.

4. Heat a large sauté pan over medium heat and add the olive oil. Add the minced shallot and stir for 1 minute, cooking the shallot.

5. Drop the farfalle into boiling water and cook for 7 minutes or until al dente, stirring occasionally.

6. Add the tomatoes to the sauté pan, and cook for 1 minute.

7. Strain the pasta, allowing all of the water to drain off, and add the pasta to the pan with the sauce along with the chopped basil. Mix the pasta in with the sauce and adjust the seasoning with salt and pepper. Serve immediately topped with the freshly grated Parmesan cheese.

SHAPING THE RAVIOLI

1. Follow the instructions for rolling out the pasta dough in the "Shaping the Pasta" section on page 209. Roll the dough out to setting 6.

2. Lay the dough out on a floured (semolina) work surface and use a 3-inch round serrated cutter to cut out as many rounds as you can. Have a small bowl available with about half a cup of warm water in it. Wet your index fingertip in the bowl and gently brush the outside circumference of the circle.

3. Place 1 teaspoon of the desired filling in the center of the circle that is wet and place another circle on top of the filling. Work your way around the ravioli,

4. Place the ravioli in a single layer on a baking sheet dusted with semolina while you finish with the remaining circles. *Raviolis freeze well. I normally place the entire baking sheet in the freezer to allow the raviolis to freeze individually and then transfer them to freezer bags to be stored for up to 3 months.*

The Atlas pasta machine has an attachment to make ravioli. The ravioli from the machine are square and can be produced rather quickly. The basic process involves feeding two sheets of dough through the attachment with the filling sandwiched between the two layers. Instructions are included with the attachment. Atlas pasta machines and various attachments can be purchased from most kitchenware stores or catalogs.

Sweet Potato Ravioli with a Pine Nut and Sage Butter Sauce

FILLS ABOUT 50 RAVIOLIS

TWO 1-POUND SWEET POTATOES
SPLASH OF EXTRA VIRGIN OLIVE OIL
KOSHER SALT AND BLACK PEPPER
2 TABLESPOONS UNSALTED BUTTER, SOFT
2 TABLESPOONS BROWN SUGAR, FIRMLY PACKED
1 BATCH EGG PASTA DOUGH (RECIPE, PAGE 208)
1 TEASPOON CANOLA OIL
2 LARGE SHALLOTS, MINCED
1/4 CUP UNSALTED BUTTER
8 LARGE FRESH SAGE LEAVES (RESERVE 4 WHOLE LEAVES
    FOR GARNISH), THINLY SLICED
1/2 TEASPOON CRUSHED RED PEPPER FLAKES
1/4 CUP PINE NUTS, TOASTED
KOSHER SALT AND WHITE PEPPER

1. Preheat the oven to 400 degrees.

2. To make the filling, cut the sweet potatoes in half lengthwise, brush with olive oil and season with kosher salt and black pepper. Place cut side down on a baking sheet and roast until tender, about 50 minutes. Cool for 5 minutes, then

scoop the pulp out of the potato skins and into a small bowl. Discard the skins.

3. Add soft butter and brown sugar and mash well.

4. Roll the Egg pasta dough out as detailed on page 209, and follow the steps for making ravioli on page 215, using 1 teaspoon of the sweet potato filling for each ravioli.

5. Working in batches, cook the ravioli in a pot of boiling salted water until tender, about 4–5 minutes if fresh, or 7–9 minutes if frozen. Drain well.

6. To make the pine nut and sage butter sauce, heat the canola oil in a large sauté pan over medium heat. Sauté the shallots for 2 minutes, stirring. Add the butter and brown slightly, about 3 minutes. Remove from the heat and add the sage, red pepper flakes and pine nuts. Season to taste with salt and white pepper.

7. Add the ravioli to the pan with the butter sauce and toss to coat. Transfer to plates, drizzling any remaining sauce from the pan over the ravioli. Garnish plates with whole sage leaves and serve immediately.

The three pasta dough recipes that I provide in this cookbook will give you confidence in making various flavored doughs. Once you feel comfortable with these three recipes, you can advance to other flavor combinations like black pepper pasta, herb pasta (using parsley and other herbs in place of spinach), tomato (using tomato paste in place of beets), lemon–pepper pasta (using finely minced lemon zest and ground black pepper). The possibilities are endless—just make sure that everything you add to the dough is finely minced or pureed or the dough will fall apart when you begin to work with it. ∎

Green Pea Ravioli with Lemon and Olive Oil

In the spring when green peas hit the market, I find myself shucking pounds of them to create these wonderful ravioli. The fresh lemon and olive oil sauce complements but never overpowers their delicate flavor. ■

FILLS ABOUT 50 RAVIOLIS

2 CUPS BABY PEAS, FRESH OR FROZEN
1 LARGE SHALLOT, MINCED
2 TEASPOONS EXTRA VIRGIN OLIVE OIL
1/2 CUP FRESHLY GRATED PARMESAN CHEESE
1/2 CUP BREAD CRUMBS
1/2 TEASPOON KOSHER SALT
2 PINCHES WHITE PEPPER
1 BATCH EGG PASTA DOUGH (RECIPE, PAGE 208)

1. Puree the peas in a food processor. Place the pea puree in a medium-sized bowl.

2. In a small sauté pan set over medium heat, sauté the shallots in the olive oil until they become translucent. Remove from the heat and stir into the pea puree with the cheese and breadcrumbs. Season with salt and white pepper.

3. Roll the Egg pasta dough out as detailed on page 209, and follow the steps for making ravioli on page 215, using 1 teaspoon of the green pea filling for each ravioli.

Lemon and Olive Oil Sauce

2 CLOVES GARLIC, MINCED
1/4 CUP EXTRA VIRGIN OLIVE OIL
JUICE FROM 1/2 LEMON
2 TEASPOONS FRESHLY GRATED LEMON ZEST
1/2 CUP CHICKEN STOCK
KOSHER SALT AND WHITE PEPPER
1 TEASPOON SNIPPED CHIVES

1. Heat a large sauté pan over medium heat. Sauté the minced garlic in the olive oil for 1 minute.

2. Working in batches, cook the ravioli in a pot of boiling salted water until tender, about 4–5 minutes if fresh, or 7–9 minutes if frozen. Drain well.

3. Add the lemon juice, lemon zest and chicken stock. Season with salt and white pepper. Toss in the snipped chives at the last minute.

4. Add the ravioli to the pan with the lemon sauce and toss to coat. Transfer the raviolis to plates and drizzle any remaining sauce from the pan over the raviolis. Serve immediately.

Three-Cheese Tortellini with Chicken and Pesto

Tortellini Filling

FILLS ABOUT 50 RAVIOLIS

1 CUP RICOTTA CHEESE
1/2 CUP GRATED PARMESAN CHEESE
1/2 CUP GRATED ASIAGO CHEESE
1 EGG YOLK
1/2 CUP PANKO BREAD CRUMBS
KOSHER SALT AND WHITE PEPPER TO TASTE
1 BATCH SPINACH PASTA DOUGH (RECIPE, PAGE 208)

1. Mix all the filling ingredients together until well combined.

2. Roll the Spinach pasta dough out as detailed on page 209.

3. Lay the dough out on a floured (semolina) work surface and use a 3-inch

round serrated cutter to cut out as many rounds as you can. Have a small bowl available with about half a cup warm water in it. Wet your index fingertip in the bowl and gently brush the outside circumference of the circle.

4. Place $^1/_2$ teaspoon of the three-cheese filling in the center of the circle and fold the circle in half, forming a half-moon shape. Work your way around the half-moon, patting the edges together to work out any air pockets. With the flat side of the half-moon facing you, lightly wet one corner and with both hands, bring the two corners toward you and pinch together, forming and securing the tortellini.

5. Place the tortellini in a single layer on a baking sheet dusted with semolina while you finish with the remaining circles.

PESTO

2 LARGE BUNCHES FRESH BASIL (4 CUPS WHOLE BASIL LEAVES)
4 CLOVES GARLIC, MINCED
$^2/_3$ CUP EXTRA VIRGIN OLIVE OIL
$^2/_3$ CUP GRATED PARMESAN CHEESE
$^1/_4$ CUP PINE NUTS
KOSHER SALT AND FRESHLY GROUND BLACK PEPPER TO TASTE

1. Place all the Pesto ingredients in a food processor and blend until almost smooth. Season the Pesto with salt and pepper.

CHICKEN AND SAUCE

2 BONELESS AND SKINLESS CHICKEN BREASTS, THINLY SLICED
KOSHER SALT AND FRESHLY GROUND BLACK PEPPER TO TASTE
2 TABLESPOONS EXTRA VIRGIN OLIVE OIL
1 CUP CHICKEN STOCK
PINE NUTS AND FRESHLY GRATED PARMESAN CHEESE TO FINISH

There is nothing like homemade pesto. Every fall, just before the last frost, we harvest all of the basil from the herb garden and make a large batch of pesto. Traditionally, pesto is made with basil and pine nuts; however, a few alterations will offer you some unique results. Try cilantro in place of the basil and/or cashews in place of the pine nuts. Experiment with different herbs and nuts. Pesto freezes well for up to 6 months. Freeze in ice cube trays and transfer the frozen cubes to freezer bags.

1. Season the chicken breasts with salt and pepper. Sauté the chicken in a hot sauté pan with the olive oil. Cook over medium heat, stirring, until cooked through and golden browned, about 2 minutes.

2. Working in batches, cook the tortellini in a pot of boiling salted water until tender, about 4 minutes if fresh, or 7 minutes if frozen. Drain well.

3. Add chicken stock and Pesto to the pan and reduce the heat to low. Add the tortellini to the pan with the Pesto and toss to coat.

4. Transfer to plates, drizzling any remaining sauce from the pan over the tortellini. Sprinkle with pine nuts and freshly grated Parmesan cheese. Serve immediately.

My Goat cheese and beet salad is a vibrantly colored and flavored dish. It is a great salad to prepare ahead of time and take to a potluck, picnic or friend's house. It is equally impressive served on fine china as a starter to a five-course meal. If you don't care for the taste of goat cheese, substitute this filling with the Three-cheese filling from the tortellini recipe. ■

GOAT CHEESE AND BEET RAVIOLI SALAD

GOAT CHEESE FILLING

FILLS ABOUT 25 RAVIOLIS

⅓ CUP GOAT CHEESE
3 TABLESPOONS GRATED PARMESAN CHEESE
1 EGG YOLK
2 TABLESPOONS PANKO BREAD CRUMBS
KOSHER SALT AND WHITE PEPPER TO TASTE
1 BATCH BEET PASTA DOUGH (RECIPE, PAGE 209)

1. Mix all the filling ingredients together until well combined.

2. Roll the Beet pasta dough out as detailed on page 209 and follow the steps for making ravioli on page 215, using 1 teaspoon of the goat cheese filling for each ravioli.

CHAMPAGNE VINAIGRETTE

¼ CUP CHAMPAGNE VINEGAR
2 TEASPOONS DIJON MUSTARD
1 SHALLOT, FINELY MINCED
½ TEASPOON GRANULATED SUGAR
½ CUP CANOLA OIL
¼ CUP EXTRA VIRGIN OLIVE OIL
KOSHER SALT AND WHITE PEPPER TO TASTE

1. For the vinaigrette, combine the vinegar, mustard, minced shallot and sugar in a blender and blend for 30 seconds. With the blender still running, drizzle the

2 oils in through the top hole of the blender, slowly, until combined. Stop the blender, taste and adjust the seasoning with salt and white pepper.

SALAD

> 2 POUNDS COOKING PUMPKIN
> 2 TABLESPOONS EXTRA VIRGIN OLIVE OIL
> KOSHER SALT AND FRESHLY GROUND BLACK PEPPER
> 1 POUND FRESH BEETS
> 3 BOSC PEARS
> 2 TABLESPOONS COARSELY CHOPPED ITALIAN PARSLEY

1. Preheat the oven to 350 degrees.

French & Brawn Market Place

A LOCAL INSTITUTION, French & Brawn Market Place sits on what's called the "Camden corner." The intersection of Elm Street and Mechanic Street is home to the bank, the post office and the warm, bustling market at French & Brawn, which has been providing groceries to the community since 1868. Owner Todd Anderson continues the tradition of provisioning the windjammers that frequent Camden Harbor from a summer store on the Wayfarer dock, complete with dedicated personnel and delivery service. On land, French & Brawn splits its inventory between basic grocery items and fine foods and wines. Baked goods, seafood, deli items, choice cuts of meat, exquisite cheeses and fresh herbs—not to mention good, hot coffee and stacks of the day's newspapers—draw locals to the market year-round. In fact, French & Brawn's reputation for quality is so strong that local restaurateurs, including Michael, use it as a secondary supplier, to fill in what they can't or don't want to buy elsewhere.

2. Peel and seed the pumpkin. Reserve $1/4$ cup of the pumpkin seeds. Wash the seeds and dry them. Cut the pumpkin into 1-inch chunks. Spread the pumpkin out on a small baking sheet and rub with most of the olive oil. Season with salt and pepper and roast for 20 minutes in the center of the preheated oven. On a separate baking sheet, drizzle the remaining olive oil on the pumpkin seeds and season them with salt and pepper. Toast in the oven until lightly browned. Cool both the pumpkin and the seeds and reserve.

3. Cut the greens from the top of the beets, wash them and place them in a saucepan with their skins on. Cover the beets with cold water, bring to a boil and reduce to a simmer. Cook until the beets are fork tender. Smaller beets will cook quicker. Plunge the beets into cold water for a few minutes to cool, and then work off the skins with your hands. Cut the beets into 1 inch pieces, wedges or halves, depending on their original size.

4. Cook the raviolis in a large pot of boiling water for about 4–5 minutes if fresh, or 7–9 minutes if frozen. Remove to a bowl filled with ice water to stop the cooking and set the color. Cool for 2 minutes in the water, remove and allow the raviolis to dry.

5. To serve, cut the Bosc pears in half. With a melon baller, remove the core and stem from the pears. Slice each half into 6 wedges.

6. Place pear wedges in a large bowl and coat with $1/4$ cup of the Champagne vinaigrette. Add the pumpkin, beets, chopped Italian parsley and remaining vinaigrette. Toss well to coat. Add the cooked raviolis and gently toss them in. Sprinkle with the toasted pumpkin seeds and serve at room temperature.

H

Thai Cuisine

I WAS FIRST introduced to Thai cooking while working in an Asian-fusion restaurant in Palm Springs, California, and was totally captivated by its fresh tastes and lightness. Thai cuisine perfectly combines ingredients like mint, coconut, lemongrass, lime leaves, chilies, seafood, tropical fruits, fish sauce, shrimp paste and rice, resulting in a cuisine that emphasizes balance and harmony, blending the spicy, the subtle, the sweet and the sour.

Traditional Thai cuisine consisted of seafood, rice, vegetables and herbs. Very little meat was used. The ingredients were generally boiled, steamed or most often grilled, particularly popular because of the abundance of natural wood available for cooking in Thailand. As Chinese immigrants moved to Thailand, they brought their cooking tools, including the wok and bamboo steamer, and their cooking methods, stir-frying and deep-frying. When the Portuguese introduced chilies and coconut milk to Thailand, the Thai quickly adopted these ingredients as their own. Other influences came from India and the Western cooking methods of France and England.

True Thai cooking utilizes unique ingredients that can be difficult to find such as kaffir lime leaves and galangal. The recipes I have created for the Thai cooking classes don't require these hard-to-find products and rely on more readily available ingredients. A visit to a nearby Asian market can be an education in itself—explore the various canned and dried products on the shelves, the fresh produce in the coolers and the array of frozen products unique to cuisines of this region. If you are not fortunate enough to have an Asian market nearby, don't fret. I have provided information on a few reliable Internet markets that specialize in Asian products, with very reasonable prices and shipping rates. See the list of sources on page 243. Once you have the staple products on hand and prepare some of my Thai recipes, I'm sure you will agree how simple and flavorful Thai cuisine, prepared at home, can be.

*T*HAI
CUISINE

Coconut Chicken Soup with Curry

SERVES 6–8

In the restaurant, I create two wonderful versions of this soup. The first version is given here, made with chicken. The other version is made with fresh mussels. After you infuse the wine with the lemongrass as in step 1, place it in a large stockpot and bring it to a boil. Add 3 pounds of cleaned fresh mussels and steam, covered, for about 8 minutes, or until the mussels open. Cool and pick the meat from the shells. Strain off the liquid and reserve, following the remaining instructions, adding the mussels where it calls for chicken. ▪

1 STALK LEMON GRASS
1½ CUPS DRY WHITE WINE
1 MEDIUM YELLOW ONION, FINELY CHOPPED
4 GARLIC CLOVES, MINCED
1½ TABLESPOONS FINELY GRATED PEELED FRESH GINGER
2 TABLESPOONS CANOLA OIL
1 CUP FRESH ORANGE JUICE
½ CUP FRESH LIME JUICE
2 TEASPOONS CURRY POWDER
1 TEASPOON CHOPPED FRESH THYME LEAVES
1 BAY LEAF
2 CANS UNSWEETENED COCONUT MILK (14 OUNCES EACH)
1 FRESH JALAPEÑO PEPPER, FINELY CHOPPED
1 TABLESPOON SAMBAL OELEK (HOT CHILI PASTE)
1 POUND CHICKEN BREAST, SKINLESS AND BONELESS, SLICED THINLY
2 PLUM TOMATOES, SEEDED, AND CUT INTO ½-INCH DICE
KOSHER SALT
3 TABLESPOONS CHOPPED FRESH CILANTRO
CILANTRO SPRIGS FOR GARNISH

1. Slice the lemon grass thinly and place in a small saucepan with the white wine. Cook over medium-high heat for 5 minutes to infuse the lemon flavor into the wine. Strain and reserve the wine, discarding the lemon grass.

2. In a large (4- or 5-quart) saucepan, cook the onion, garlic, and ginger in the canola oil over moderately low heat, stirring frequently, until the onion is softened.

3. Add the reserved wine, orange and lime juice, curry powder, thyme, bay leaf, coconut milk, jalapeño pepper and sambal oelek. Simmer uncovered about 15 minutes, stirring occasionally, until reduced slightly.

4. Add the sliced chicken and diced tomatoes and cook, covered, over medium-high heat for 3 minutes.

5. Season the soup with salt and add the chopped cilantro. Divide the soup between the bowls. Garnish with cilantro sprigs.

I learned this dish from a Thai cook named "Mr. Mike," many years ago. We often ate it as "family meal" before a long night on the cooking line. Thai beef salad is served family-style on a platter and is a hands-on dish to eat. The correct way to eat this salad is for everyone to take a bibb lettuce leaf and fill it with some of the beef mixture. Then add a tomato wedge, a slice of cucumber, more mint or another squeeze of lime, roll it up and eat it like you would a taco.

GRILLED THAI BEEF SALAD

SERVES 4

1 POUND BEEF TENDERLOIN (TRIMMED)
2 TEASPOONS FRESH LIME JUICE
2 TEASPOONS FISH SAUCE
1 TABLESPOON CANOLA OIL
KOSHER SALT AND FRESHLY GROUND BLACK PEPPER
2 TABLESPOONS UNCOOKED JASMINE RICE
2 LIMES
¼ CUP FISH SAUCE
2 SHALLOTS, FINELY SLICED
1 TABLESPOON FINELY CHOPPED CILANTRO
2 SCALLIONS, GREEN PART ONLY, THINLY SLICED ON BIAS
2 TABLESPOONS SLICED FRESH SPEARMINT LEAVES
1 JALAPEÑO PEPPER, STEM AND SEEDS REMOVED
    AND THINLY SLICED
2 HEADS BIBB LETTUCE
½ SMALL CUCUMBER, THINLY SLICED
1 VINE RIPE TOMATO, CORED AND CUT INTO WEDGES
4 SPRIGS FRESH SPEARMINT

1. Slice the beef into 1-inch thick medallions. Sprinkle with lime juice, fish sauce, oil, salt and pepper. Let stand for 10 minutes to marinate.

2. Grill the beef until it is medium rare, and allow it to rest for 10 minutes.

3. In a small dry frying pan, toast the rice until the grains turn light brown. When toasted, place the rice in a mortar and pestle or spice grinder and crush. Take one of the limes and cut into 4 wedges and remove the central membranes. Thinly slice one of the wedges width-wise, including the peel and flesh. Reserve the remaining wedges for garnish.

4. In a large bowl, combine the sliced lime, the juice of the other lime, fish sauce, shallots, cilantro, scallions, mint and jalapeño. Thinly slice the beef and add to the bowl along with the toasted rice. Mix well.

5. When ready to serve, arrange the cleaned bibb lettuce leaves on half the platter and decoratively place the beef salad on the other half. Garnish with tomato wedges, sliced cucumber, mint sprigs and lime wedges.

Spicy Cucumber Salad with Roasted Peanuts

SERVES 4

1/4 CUP WHOLE PEANUTS (UNSALTED)
2 ENGLISH CUCUMBERS (SEEDLESS), THINLY SLICED
3 SHALLOTS, THINLY SLICED
2 JALAPEÑO PEPPERS, STEMS AND SEEDS REMOVED AND THINLY SLICED
1/4 RED BELL PEPPER, JULIENNE
3 TABLESPOONS COARSELY CHOPPED FRESH SPEARMINT
1/4 CUP FRESH LIME JUICE

Spicy Cucumber Salad is a refreshing and easy salad to make. It is made with an ingredient called fish sauce, also known as "nam pla" in Thailand or "nuoc nam" in Vietnam. Fish sauce is made from salted and fermented fish, which produces a liquid that has a very distinguished and pungent aroma with a salty flavor. Fish sauce is a staple ingredient throughout Southeast Asia. ■

2 TABLESPOONS FISH SAUCE
2 TABLESPOONS PALM SUGAR (OR SUBSTITUTE BROWN SUGAR)
2 GARLIC CLOVES, MINCED
KOSHER SALT AND FRESHLY GROUND BLACK PEPPER

1. Place the peanuts in a shallow baking dish and roast in a 350-degree oven for 10 minutes.

2. Combine the cucumbers, shallots, jalapeño, red bell pepper and mint in a bowl.

3. In another small bowl, whisk together the lime juice, fish sauce, palm sugar and garlic.

4. Add the dressing to the cucumbers and toss to coat. Season to taste with salt and freshly ground black pepper. Garnish with the roasted peanuts and serve.

CRAB SPRING ROLLS WITH A SWEET CHILI-PEANUT SAUCE

SERVES 4

6 SHEETS ROUND RICE PAPER
1/2 POUND FRESH CRABMEAT
1 LARGE CARROT, SHREDDED
2 OUNCES BABY SPINACH
3 SCALLIONS, GREEN PART ONLY, SLICED THINLY
KOSHER SALT AND BLACK PEPPER TO TASTE

1. Place the rice paper sheets on a flat surface and brush with a little warm water. Let them sit for a few minutes to absorb the water and become pliable. If they are still hard in places, brush with a little more water.

Fresh spring rolls can be made with any number of fillings. A vegetarian filling can be made using the carrot, baby spinach and scallions, and adding tiny pieces of blanched broccoli, bean sprouts or sliced, blanched snow peas. Cooked shredded pork, chicken or duck meat also works well in place of the crabmeat as does sliced cooked shrimp or lobster meat. The possibilities are endless.

2. Divide the crabmeat, shredded carrots, baby spinach and scallions between the 6 rounds of rice paper, placing a pile at the front of the sheets. The tricky part of rolling these spring rolls is to roll them tightly without tearing the rice paper, so take your time. Starting with the front edge of the rice paper, roll it up over the filling and continue rolling it up $^3/_4$ of the way. Bring the sides in to enclose the filling and finish rolling it the rest of the way.

3. Keep covered with moist paper towels until serving. Serve with the Sweet chili peanut sauce (recipe follows).

SWEET CHILI-PEANUT SAUCE

1 CUP SWEET CHILI SAUCE
2 TEASPOONS COARSELY CHOPPED FRESH CILANTRO
2 TABLESPOONS COARSELY CHOPPED ROASTED PEANUTS (UNSALTED)
2 TABLESPOONS RICE WINE VINEGAR

1. Combine all the ingredients and mix well. *Keep the sauce covered in the refrigerator, for up to 1 week.*

THAI NOODLE SALAD WITH CHICKEN

SERVES 4

ONE 6-OUNCE PACKAGE $^1/_4$-INCH RICE STICKS
2 TABLESPOONS CANOLA OIL
2 BONELESS AND SKINLESS CHICKEN BREAST HALVES, SMALL DICE
$^1/_4$ CUP THINLY SLICED SCALLIONS, GREEN PART ONLY
$^1/_4$ CUP COARSELY CHOPPED FRESH CILANTRO
1 CUP SWEET CHILI SAUCE
3 TABLESPOONS RICE WINE VINEGAR

Thai noodle salad is a great starter to a Thai-theme meal. This salad is so versatile and any number of ingredients can be used in place of the chicken breast. Some alternatives are grilled chicken breast, grilled shrimp, cooked lobster meat, seared scallops or vegetables such as blanched broccoli florets or red bell peppers cut into $^1/_2$-inch pieces. ▪

¹/₄ CUP COARSELY CHOPPED ROASTED PEANUTS (UNSALTED)
WHOLE ROASTED PEANUTS AND FRESH CILANTRO SPRIGS
FOR GARNISH

1. Place the rice sticks in a large bowl. Cover with cold water and let sit until the noodles begin to soften, about 10 minutes. Drain off the water

2. In a large pot of boiling water, cook the noodles until just tender and pliable, about 3 minutes. Drain in a colander and rinse with cold water to cool. Drain off all excess water from the noodles until they are rather dry, and place them in a large bowl.

3. In a medium-sized sauté pan, heat the canola oil over medium-high heat. When hot, add the diced chicken breasts and cook, stirring constantly until cooked through.

4. Place the cooked chicken in with the noodles and add the remaining ingredients. Toss to blend. Garnish with cilantro sprigs and whole roasted peanuts.

Chicken Satay with Peanut Sauce

MAKES 30 SATAYS

3 CHICKEN BREASTS, BONELESS AND SKINLESS (1¹/₂ POUNDS)
1 TABLESPOON SOY SAUCE
1 TEASPOON CURRY POWDER
10-INCH BAMBOO SKEWERS (SOAK IN WATER)

1. Thinly slice the chicken breast lengthwise into long ¹/₄-inch thick strips. A chicken breast that weighs ¹/₂ pound will yield about 10 slices. Weave the strips onto the bamboo skewers, one long strip per skewer, spreading them out to

Satay (also spelled saté) is actually an Indonesian specialty and can be made with any number of meats from chicken and pork to beef and shrimp. The meats are simply sliced or cubed and threaded onto bamboo skewers. The meat is then marinated, grilled and served with a peanut sauce. ▪

cover about half the skewer. Lay them on a platter and sprinkle with soy sauce and curry powder. Marinate for 10 minutes.

2. Heat a barbeque grill or grill pan over high heat and grill the skewers on each side for 1 minute or until cooked through. Serve with warm Peanut sauce (recipe follows).

PEANUT SAUCE

1/4 CUP CANOLA OIL
4 CLOVES GARLIC, MINCED
4 MEDIUM SHALLOTS, CHOPPED
1 TEASPOON CRUSHED RED PEPPER
1 TEASPOON CURRY POWDER
1/2 TEASPOON GROUND CUMIN
1/2 TEASPOON GROUND CORIANDER
2 CUPS UNSWEETENED COCONUT MILK
1 CUP WHOLE MILK
1/4 CUP LIME JUICE
2 BAY LEAVES
1/4 CUP FISH SAUCE
1/4 CUP DARK BROWN SUGAR, FIRMLY PACKED
2 CUPS CHUNKY PEANUT BUTTER

1. Heat a 4-quart saucepan over medium heat. Add the oil and sauté the garlic, shallots, crushed red pepper, curry, cumin and coriander for 3 minutes.

2. Stir in the coconut milk, milk, lime juice, bay leaves, fish sauce, brown sugar and peanut butter. Stir well. Reduce the heat to medium-low and continue to cook, stirring frequently, until the sauce thickens, about 25 minutes.

3. Remove bay leaves and serve.

Peanut sauce is the traditional accompaniment to satay. While it is rather rich, I have also served it as a sauce on everything from grilled chicken breast to filet mignon. Peanut sauce is also a nice dip to serve warm with blanched vegetables.

Red Curry of Maine Lobster with Shrimp and Pineapple

SERVES 4

2 TABLESPOONS THAI RED CURRY PASTE (RECIPE FOLLOWS)
TWO 1¼ POUND LIVE MAINE LOBSTERS
12 EXTRA-LARGE RAW SHRIMP, PEELED AND DEVEINED
5 TABLESPOONS TAMARIND
1 TABLESPOON PALM SUGAR (OR SUBSTITUTE BROWN SUGAR)
½ CUP COCONUT CREAM (COCO LOPEZ)
2 TABLESPOONS FISH SAUCE
ONE 14-OUNCE CAN UNSWEETENED COCONUT MILK
ONE 15-OUNCE CAN STRAW MUSHROOMS, STRAINED
2 CUPS STRINGED AND JULIENNE SNOW PEAS
1 CUP ½-INCH DICE FRESH PINEAPPLE
¼ CUP COARSELY CHOPPED CILANTRO
1 BATCH STEAMED RICE (RECIPE, PAGE 240)

1. In a large 9-quart stockpot with lid, boil 1 gallon of water. At the boil, add the lobsters and replace the lid. Boil for 10 minutes. Remove the lobsters from the pot and cool. *Reserve the liquid.*

2. Cut the lobsters in half lengthwise and remove the meat from the claws, knuckles and tails (discarding the vein). Cut the lobster meat into 1-inch (large, bite-sized) pieces. Reserve the meat. Clean out the lobster body cavity and reserve for presentation.

3. Bring 2 cups of the lobster cooking water to a boil, remove from the heat and add the tamarind and palm sugar. Steep for 3 minutes, breaking them up to dissolve them. Strain the tamarind liquid and reserve.

Coconut milk is packaged in cans and is widely available in Asian markets and often in local supermarkets. Coconut milk is made by combining equal parts of shredded coconut and water, then simmering and straining the mixture to extract all of the flavors from the coconut. Be careful not to confuse coconut milk with sweetened coconut cream such as Coco Lopez, which is very sweet, and suitable for very different purposes.

4. Boil the coconut cream, stirring it constantly. Add the curry paste, reducing the heat to medium and cook for 3 minutes. Add the tamarind liquid, fish sauce and coconut milk. Bring to a simmer and add the shrimp, cook for 3 minutes, stirring. Add the lobster meat, straw mushrooms, snow peas and diced pineapple. Cook for 2 more minutes. Stir in the chopped cilantro.

5. Lay the 4 lobster body halves over a bed of steamed rice. Distribute the lobster meat and shrimp between the lobster shells and ladle the remaining vegetables and sauce over the top. Serve immediately.

THAI RED CURRY PASTE

    5 DRIED LARGE RED CHILIES (DRIED NEW MEXICO CHILIES
        OR ANCHO CHILIES)
    4 SHALLOTS, PEELED
    4 CLOVES GARLIC, PEELED
    1 (QUARTER-SIZED) CHUNK OF PEELED FRESH GINGER
        (GALANGAL IF AVAILABLE), MINCED
    1 STALK LEMONGRASS, BOTTOM 6 INCHES FINELY MINCED
    1 TEASPOON LIME ZEST (KAFFIR IF AVAILABLE)
    1 TEASPOON GROUND WHITE PEPPER
    1 TEASPOON CORIANDER SEEDS, TOASTED LIGHTLY AND GROUND
    1/2 TEASPOON CUMIN SEEDS, TOASTED LIGHTLY AND GROUND
    2 TABLESPOONS SMOKED TROUT
    1 TEASPOON DRIED SHRIMP
    1 TEASPOON SALT

1. Soak the dried red chilies in warm water for 1 hour.

2. Roast the shallots and garlic in a 350-degree oven for 1 hour.

3. Place all the ingredients in a food processor and puree (adding a little water if necessary to combine).

Thai curry is completely different from the curries of India. In Thailand, curries are made from a combination of fresh ingredients (often grilled or roasted for extra flavor), chilies and dried spices, which are then added to a base of coconut milk. There are as many "correct" ways to make a Thai curry paste as there are to make an Italian marinara. ■

STEAMED RICE

2 CUPS JASMINE RICE
2 CUPS COLD WATER
1 TABLESPOON SALT

1. Rinse the rice well and drain. Find a bowl that is large enough to hold 2 quarts of water and will fit inside a large (9-quart) stockpot.

2. Pour 1 quart of water into the stockpot, along with a steamer rack or bunched aluminum foil or ramekins to keep the bowl from touching the bottom of the pot.

3. Transfer the rice to the 2-quart bowl and add the salt and cold water. Place the bowl in the pot, supported up off the bottom, and place the pot over high heat. Cover the pot and bring the water to a boil. At the boil, reduce the heat to medium and continue steaming the rice for 25 minutes.

4. Remove the bowl from the pot with a pair of tongs (be careful of the steam) and fluff the rice with a fork. Keep covered with plastic wrap until serving. Will keep hot for up to 1 hour if kept in a warm place.

COCONUT-FRIED BANANAS WITH LYCHEES AND PAPAYA

SERVES 6

1 FRESH RIPE PAPAYA
2 TABLESPOONS GRANULATED SUGAR
ORANGE JUICE AS NEEDED
6 FIRM RIPE BANANAS
3 LARGE EGGS, LIGHTLY BEATEN

Lychees are a Chinese fruit that is widely available, canned, from Asian markets. The fresh fruit is occasionally available from specialty fruit markets and is grown in subtropical regions such as Florida, California and Hawaii. The lychee (also known as litchi nut) is a small, round fruit with a very thin and rough dark skin. The flesh, which surrounds a large single seed, is creamy white and smooth and has a delicate flavor unlike that of any other fruit. ■

¼ CUP HONEY
¼ CUP ALL-PURPOSE FLOUR
2 CUPS SHREDDED COCONUT
¼ CUP UNSALTED BUTTER
2 CANS LYCHEES

1. To make the papaya sauce, remove the seeds and skin from the papaya and place in a blender with the sugar and enough orange juice to make a puree.

2. Peel the bananas and cut them in half lengthwise and then once crosswise. Mix the eggs with the honey and flour.

3. Spread the shredded coconut out on a plate. Dip the bananas into the egg mixture, coating them well, and roll them in the coconut.

4. Heat a large sauté pan over medium heat and melt the butter. Lay the bananas in the melted butter and cook slowly for 5 minutes. Turn over and cook for another 4 minutes. Add the lychees to the pan with the bananas and heat for 1 minute, tossing.

5. Distribute the bananas and lychees between the plates, stacking the bananas, and surround with a pool of the papaya sauce.

Mail Order Sources for Specialty Food Items

HOW DO YOU prepare Caribbean dishes in the middle of a Maine winter? Luckily, we have several reliable local sources for much of the tropical produce, but try to find annatto seeds in mid-coast Maine! If you're having trouble finding ingredients for any of my recipes, here's a list of reliable sources I use to get specialty products.

HARTSTONE INN MARKETPLACE: Visit us online for some of Chef Michael's specialty food products, including his Caribbean dry spice mix, bordelaise sauce base and Hartstone granola. For gift ideas and unique items for dining, Mary Jo offers everything from Portmeirion china and crystal knife rests to porcelain teapots and Pickwick teas. Also available are Hartstone Inn caps, shirts and tote bags. www.hartstoneinn.com

SPICES AND DRIED HERBS: **Penzeys** carries a great fresh assortment of both specialty and standard spices and dried herbs, including annatto seeds, Chinese five spice and crystallized ginger. 1-800-741-7787 or www.penzeys.com

GLOBAL KNIVES: **Professional Cutlery Direct** (PCD) carries the full line of Global knives (my favorite knives) as well as other great kitchen gadgets. 1-800-859-6994 or www.cutlery.com

BAKING SUPPLIES: **The Baker's Catalogue** specializes in ingredients and tools for the home baker. They carry King Arthur flours, dough starters, vanilla beans, pastry bags—basically everything you need to bake. 1-800-827-6836 or www.bakerscatalogue.com

ASIAN INGREDIENTS: I am fortunate to have a few excellent Asian markets within 1$^1/_2$ hours of the Inn, and I enjoy visiting them to see the products firsthand. If you don't have an Asian market nearby, try one or both of these online grocers:

Temple of Thai: 1-877-811-8773 or www.templeofthai.com

Pacific Island Market: 1-636-272-2746 or www.asiamex.com

LIVE MAINE LOBSTERS: Yes, you can get live Maine lobsters delivered directly to your door from a very reliable local company. **Graffam Brothers**, located in Rockport, Maine, selects the sizes and quantities you like, carefully packages and ships them to you. 1-800-535-5358 or www.lobsterstogo.com

SMOKED SEAFOOD: **Duck Trap River Fish Farms**, located in Belfast Maine, is a terrific source for smoked seafood. They offer a wide range of products from smoked scallops and mussels to smoked salmon and trout. They also have a wonderful catalog and ship anywhere. 1-800-828-3825 or www.ducktrap.com

MAINE GOAT CHEESE: **Appleton Creamery** is one of the vendors I highlight in this book. They produce an excellent goat cheese. 780 Gurney Town Road, Appleton, Maine 04862 or www.appletoncreamery.com

INDEX